FANCY PRISON

---

*Calling BS on the Child
Welfare Industry*

FANCY PRISON

Calling BS on the Child Welfare Industry

Tina Fumo

Published by Best Seller Publishing®, St. Augustine, FL
Best Seller Publishing® is a registered trademark.
Printed in the United States of America.
ISBN: 9798755179034

Cover photographs:
Mount Rundle, Banff National Park, Canada, taken by Scott Rowed
Baby Delonna Sullivan, refer to Chapter 9

This publication is designed to provide accurate and authoritative information with regard to the subject matter covered. It is sold with the understanding that the publisher is not engaged in rendering legal, accounting, or other professional advice. If legal advice or other expert assistance is required, the services of a competent professional should be sought. The opinions expressed by the authors in this book are not endorsed by Best Seller Publishing® and are the sole responsibility of the author rendering the opinion.

Copies of this publication may be purchased in bulk for use in education, business, fundraising, or sales-promotion. For information, please contact Tina Fumo at www.gentlegiants.academia.edu or contact her on Facebook or LinkedIn by searching Tina Fumo.

For more information, please write:
Best Seller Publishing®
53 Marine Street
St. Augustine, FL 32084
or call 1 (626) 765-9750
Visit us online at: www.BestSellerPublishing.org

Dedicated to my mother, Rita Fumo,
my Aunt Dianne, and Mrs. Grant,
three phenomenal women who helped shape me in my youth

CONTENTS

PROLOGUE

I promised my daughter they wouldn't take her baby.
I broke that promise for twenty-seven days.
Then I promised I would seek justice for what was done to her.
This is that second promise ...

Canadian winters are known the world over to be extremely cold and harsh. On March 8, 2017—it was a Wednesday—that general fact was certainly true. I'd left my home at 5 a.m., with my destination being this shithole town in the province of British Columbia. My daughter had been living there for the past few years and, for the most part, hadn't done so well. Ever since she was a little girl, she'd had trouble with transitions, so this trip was Mom's gentle nudging, urging her to move on. She had just given birth to a baby girl and needed a fresh start as a new mother.

The blizzard I'd been dealing with since the wee hours of the morning was causing my knuckles to turn white as I gripped the steering wheel. My back was hunched, bent over it, with my bifocals oscillating up and down. I was trying to see through the snow whipping across my high beams and focus on not losing that road and driving into a ditch.

A trip that would have normally taken two-and-a-half hours took over four. I drove past Banff, which had been my home for thirty years. I pulled over and texted my husband, who had been very worried about me, knowing that I'd left while he was still sleeping. I let my husband know that I was fine and that I was just heading west past Banff. I told him I thought I was through the worst of the storm and to let our friend know as well; she had reached out with concern.

I still had about five or six hours of driving ahead of me, so my rest break was over. And though I'd just made it through the morning's winter blizzard, the "storm" I was heading into would be far worse.

Our Baby, Our World

1

OUR BABY

What prompted this road trip was a call from my long-time friend, Suzanne. She called me when my grand-baby was ten days old. Her exact words were "Tina, get here now. In my experience, it's a lot more difficult to get children back after they've been put in foster care."

Get our baby back!? Foster care!? What the hell was going on? I was heeding Suzanne's advice and I wanted to hold my grandchild.

My daughter didn't know I was coming. Suzanne had been her constant companion and support since the baby[1] was born.

My daughter had asked Suzanne to be there in a doula capacity, so Suzanne had stayed in the hospital room with her. There was a lot of commotion and stress with the Ministry of Child and

---

[1]   *I call my grandchild "baby" throughout these starting scenes. So much of what the Ministry of Child and Family Development (MCFD)/Child Protection Services (CPS) does is utter confusion, it is intentional on my part not to name her. I address it later.*

Family Development (MCFD)[2] involved in the situation. The baby even had an ankle monitor put on her tiny body that would set off alarms every time Suzanne wandered too far from the nursing station. This bugged Suzanne immensely and distressed my daughter beyond words. I didn't know why any of this was occurring. Getting my daughter's situation sorted was my sole motivation for the trip, and that's all I could focus on.

Suzanne phoned me when she realized her presence there wasn't going to matter. She had briefly returned to her home in Vancouver when the baby was about a week old. She went home, turned around, and came right back to my daughter and her child. Suzanne packed enough to stay for a month, but she hadn't seen my daughter's residence yet.

It was a shithole house in a shithole town. The rent was cheap for my daughter—it was really all she could afford as a single mom—but it would've had to have been, considering what a horrid residence it was. My granddaughter would not be growing up there (in that house and that town) if I had anything to say about it. I didn't realize then how vital Suzanne would become to us in the days and weeks ahead.

When Suzanne did see what would be her temporary home with my daughter, she was disgusted too. I had tried to warn her, but my words hadn't adequately described the physical state the house was in.

Fortunately, Suzanne had only stayed there for a couple of nights before calling me when the baby was ten days old. I dropped everything in my life to help my daughter make a transition, with the number one priority being better housing. Ironically enough, deeming this shithole house as acceptable accommodation for a new mom and her baby was the *one* thing

---

[2] *The Ministry of Child and Family Development (MCFD) is the government department of Child Protection Services (CPS) in the Canadian province of British Columbia. The MCFD and CPS are one and the same, although the different acronyms used for each province/state/territory contribute to the overall confusion.*

that the MCFD had signed off on at that point (of their systematic routine of setting up a new mom to fail!).

After leaving my home at 5 a.m. and dealing with a blizzard, I was too tired and confused to navigate even the tiniest streets when I arrived in town. Suzanne was going to tell my daughter she was taking the baby for a walk. I was waiting at the first coffee shop I saw when I arrived and, it turned out, it was just a few short blocks for Suzanne to get to me. I was dressed like a vagabond, so I fit right in with the local flavour, having dressed that morning for comfort over fashion. My grandbaby wouldn't remember what I was wearing the first time I saw her—nor would she care.

When Suzanne arrived, my granddaughter wailed at being taken out of her swaddling. Remembering once again the moment of birth when a wrinkly baby squished out of me, I was in shock and awe at what tiny beings we are when we start out in life. I lay my granddaughter out on the table on her blankets so I could get a good look at her and caress her tiny hands. Suzanne waited in line to get coffee and answered questions from strangers as to the crying lady with the baby on the table.

"It's the grandmother," she said. People just nodded in understanding.

I swaddled the baby and settled her down. I needed caffeine and wanted to hear the minute-to-minute updates on the situation, which was fluid. I'd had none of my calls to the social worker returned while I was driving there.

After Suzanne filled me in as best she could, we went to get my daughter. I was shocked at how thin she was, despite having just given birth. She was surprised to see me, and there was something more: for a split second, I saw an expression of hers that I knew well. It said to me, "What next?"

My heart broke a little, as this is not the maternal bliss new moms are supposed to be in.

I told my daughter to pack a few things and that we were going to a hotel. Her eyes lit up instantly and she and Suzanne went to get their things. I waited in the car as they put suitcases, a diaper bag, and other stuff in the trunk. My daughter asked,

"For how long?" but I remained vague and said we'd discuss it at the hotel. I didn't want to see her housemates, and I didn't want them to hear our conversation.

If I had known then what I know now, the answer to my daughter's question would have been, "A month." And I would never be the same person again.

When we got to the hotel and settled into our room, I, too, wondered, *How long?* The nightly rate certainly wasn't cheap. Perhaps staying in a room with two other people is fun on vacation, but this wasn't that. I didn't know *what* this was, as I still hadn't heard back from the social worker. I'd let her know in a message that I was staying in town and what hotel we were at.

That particular social worker came to be known as "winky-face Kathy" due to her prolific use of the winky-face emoticon after each text with my daughter. Her texts to me, when she finally did start returning my messages, were missing this annoying graphic.

When I remember those days in first the fancy hotel, then the cheaper one, it makes me chuckle. We must've changed hotels and rooms three or four times over the next month, and every time we would check in, I'd need to first use the bathroom.

By the time I had finished relieving myself and washing up, I'd come out to see a changing area already set up, with a soft mat on whatever counter space was in the room and newborn clothes and diapers neatly stacked next to it. It was the first thing my daughter unpacked, ready for the next soiled diaper.

The three of us unwound a bit in various stages of unpacking and setting toiletries in the bathroom. We chatted as we did, and my daughter realized I was there to help her find a more suitable residence for her and her baby. She was okay with that. The house she was living in was disgusting—and not by her doing. She had a small area allotted to her and her baby. Her bedroom had barely enough room for a dresser, and a windowless corner for the change table in the basement served as the nursery. Upstairs lived a family with four children, and there was another "tenant" in a basement bedroom down the hall from my daughter's bedroom. She shared a bathroom. On previous visits, I had always seemed to find dog shit in it from the family's canine, which had the run of the place, along with their four children, who always seemed in various stages of dress and undress.

I had no desire to "visit" them as I had done in the past. I didn't know what the hell was going on, but I'd had a bad feeling about the parents of these four children. I couldn't quite put my finger on it, but I somehow knew their involvement in my daughter's life as landlord/friends/family was contributing to the overall confusion. The living arrangement was overcrowded and chaotic. The kitchen was always messy, and my daughter didn't have a choice. There was only one kitchen, and she usually had to clean up a bit before being able to make something for herself. The parents paid rent on the whole house, and their family of six took up the main floor. That was why they were "subletting" the rooms downstairs to my daughter and this other tenant: to help them pay the full rent. They had also been dealing with the owner of the house over the expense of extermination. The house, as if it wasn't already bad enough, had a problem with mice.

It was unclear to me, now and then, whether the MCFD had signed off on this residence as being suitable, knowing that it had a serious rodent problem.

Obviously, going to the hotel was a welcome change for my daughter and her baby. The first night in there with "three women and a baby" was nothing short of magic. I had crashed sometime around 9 p.m. and slept a solid few hours before being woken by the baby's fussing. She was getting hungry, and Suzanne was bouncing her around in her arms, pacing back and forth to avoid disturbing the other hotel guests and let Mom sleep a little longer.

We did a shift change, and I tried keeping the baby quiet a little longer until it couldn't be helped. My daughter needed sleep, but obviously her baby needed feeding, too. I gently woke my daughter, placed the baby alongside her so she could suckle, and then retrieved the baby to burp her after feeding.

Suzanne and my daughter drifted off to sleep, and I was alone with my grandbaby. She was the most beautiful child I'd ever seen.

As the baby fell easily back to sleep after her burp, I placed her in the bassinet and couldn't take my eyes off her. There were two beds in the room; my daughter and Suzanne slept in one, and I had the other. I'd been going since 5 a.m. with very little sleep, yet I was wide awake. You often hear of family bonding with their baby. Well, I can tell you precisely when I started bonding with my grandchild.

It was when she slept. I set her in the bassinet, which I'd placed on the floor between the two beds. I lowered the frilly cover so I had an unobstructed view of her. Then I crawled under my covers, propped up on my side with my head resting on my hand, and watched her sleep. For hours. I got to know every detail of her face: her rosebud lips set against flawless skin, her fuzzy, soft hair, and her tiny hands clasped underneath her cheek. Her little bum stuck in the air and, it seems, she's still fond of that sleeping position. I know newborn babies are tiny, but, my word, she seemed to float just above her blankets. Her beauty and essence were so buoyant.

I don't know what time it was when she stirred for her next feeding. I repeated the routine from before and then, this time, made sure everyone was tucked in before falling asleep myself. Tomorrow was another day, still filled with confusion, and it would be the last full day we'd have with the baby for quite some time.

Since my journey on Wednesday and my arrival in town, I'd been trying to pinpoint a time to meet winky-face Kathy. We'd set a time for 2 p.m. to meet on Thursday, and no sooner did we set it than she changed it.

"Can I come in at three instead?"

Sure.

Another text sans winky-face: "How about four?"

I was starting to think this winky-face Kathy was a flake. "Sure, four o'clock then. I'll be at your office."

Right around this time, as if we didn't need any other confusion, my phone started acting up. It wouldn't hold a charge, so just before four, I left it in my car and walked toward winky-face Kathy's office. I was a bit early but anxious to get some clarification, so I waited in the lobby of the MCFD offices. And I waited.

What is going on? Why am I waiting? Isn't this supposed to be important!?

At around 4:15 p.m., the receptionist started to acknowledge my existence waiting in the lobby (probably because quitting time was coming up). I repeated[3] who I was and who I was there to meet. It was important. I would wait.

Finally, close to 4:30, I met the infamous winky-face Kathy. She was younger than I had imagined, and she sat next to me, carrying a sleeping toddler in her arms. I had no idea who the child was, and I didn't ask. It wasn't any of my business. But she could see the confusion on my face at having to conduct a quick meeting with her while she held a sleeping child. She said she'd left me a message postponing this meeting yet again. I told her my phone was dying. We agreed that I'd come back the next morning, and I left the "meeting" with no answers or clarification.

In the few days since I'd spoken to winky-face Kathy, first on the phone and now in person, I'd been given lip service to the effect that the MCFD works with families and their goal is keep mom and baby together. Seems obvious to me. I was repeatedly told this, I guess, to give me a sense of trust.

I returned the next day and, because I'd been getting the runaround, I set my fully charged phone on the table and hoped it would record properly. Looking back years later, while writing this book and knowing now what I didn't know then, that meeting was a waste of my time. All they were doing was stalling, setting us up to fail, and biding their time until Friday afternoon.

---

[3] *Every time my daughter and I would arrive at the MCFD offices, the receptionist would ask us who we were and why we were there. It was intentionally done day after day, even though the receptionist surely recognized us. It was meant to demean us, layer by layer, and strip us of our identity.*

In the mindless routine of social workers doing their CPS jobs in ministries like MCFD, Fridays are showtime. It's also suspicious how many children are suddenly in danger of being harmed by their parents at four o'clock on Friday, just before the weekend.

My daughter and I knew none of these antics before our "meeting" on Friday afternoon. I still thought the MCFD was on our side—the side of keeping mom and baby together. My daughter didn't feel the same way but trusted me. Earlier that day, we'd had a moment in the hotel room. The morning "meeting" with winky-face Kathy took place only to kill time and plant seeds of doubt in my mind. My daughter was a hot mess of emotion when I returned from that meeting. Sensing her obvious distress, I needed to reassure her. I was holding the baby and handed her to Suzanne. I sat on the bed in front of my daughter, looked her in the eye, and promised, "She is *your* baby, and they will not get her."

While we waited in the office lobby on that Friday afternoon, the social workers needed to meet with my daughter first, alone. Again, I thought they were on our side, but I still should have never allowed that to happen, certainly not without a lawyer. (I will touch on my regrets later in the book.) Our meeting had been scheduled and rescheduled for 2 p.m. It had been scheduled and rescheduled first to come without the baby and then with the baby.

These tactics were intentional. They were to keep us off-balance and, in my daughter's case, it was probably working. She'd been dealing with these people for about two months now. I had just arrived on the scene a couple of days earlier and was starting to think this whole situation was odd and flaky. I couldn't quite put my finger on it, but I just wanted this "meeting" over and done with so we could be "free to go" and I could get my daughter situated in a better living arrangement.

My daughter rejoined me after half an hour, and all three of us—grandmother, mother, and baby—were ushered into a much larger room than the one I'd been in a few hours earlier, when I'd met winky-face Kathy alone. This time, she was joined by another social worker, Cee,[4] and both of them had situated themselves at the head of a very long conference table that could seat about a dozen or more people. My daughter and I sat next to them, essentially forming a backward capital L. They were the short stroke; we were the long. The baby was sleeping beside me in her car seat on the table.

Just like the previous meeting, I set my phone on the table in front of me and hit record. This act was met with no objection from either social worker. When I reflect back on this, because those two hours will be forever etched in our memory, what happened on that Friday afternoon was the most arrogant abuse of power these people could have inflicted on us. They knew they were being recorded, yet they went ahead and did it anyway.

For the first while, I recall there was just a bit of chitchat. They asked about the unusual spelling I chose for my daughter's name and flirted with questions about my past. I wasn't under any kind of investigation, so I remember that they were cautious about asking these questions. They framed it as idle chitchat. My answers were truthful yet reticent. I was still confused as to where this was all going.

The subject of marijuana use in my past came up. My attitude then was as it is now. I thought, *So what. It's been years since I smoked a joint, and I'm not high at the moment.* Besides, marijuana is now legal in Canada, so this line of questioning is even more irrelevant now than it was then.

But I think they were just waiting for the cue of drug use to come up in the conversation. One of them left and came back with a photocopy of a bong. It was handed to me. Was it a picture of my daughter attached to the bong? No. It was just a bong, and I know what a bong is. I glanced at the photo and set it aside. I still didn't understand where this was all going.

---

[4]   *Cee is not her real name. I've decided to take the high road and not use these social workers' real names. Perhaps if I do a second edition, I will name names.*

I suppose they couldn't wait anymore. We hadn't acted in a volatile way, which is what I think they were expecting by then. I think they were expecting me to react to that picture, as if it were the tool that addicts use. I think they were waiting for me to lose my temper with my daughter and start a huge fight right in front of them.

That didn't happen.

The foster parents were on their way, so they couldn't wait anymore.

Cee announced, "We are taking the baby."

All hell broke loose.

A rush of pressure shot to my ears and I spewed out the plea, "No, no, no, no, no, no!" I had stood up while pleading these words and begged, "You're making a mistake!"

Meanwhile, my daughter had grabbed her baby and sat at the farthest corner of the long table. In one arm, she cradled her baby. In her other hand, she dialed her phone, looking for a lawyer. Many years after this day, my daughter was able to articulate what was going through her mind when the MCFD said they were taking her baby. She described "sheer panic" and flashes of the layout of the building we were in. It is a mother's primal instinct to flee with her child, so these flashes my daughter described to me made sense. She said she remembered key codes the social workers had used to get in and out of areas that led us to this room. These flashes she had were like a maze—a jigsaw puzzle to a way out she was trying to fit together. In the end, she didn't flee, of course. She stayed with me, though she could hear me begging with social workers and knew I was wasting my time.

I had raised a smart kid.

But the social workers seemed to think I had raised some piece-of-shit daughter who had no business being a mother. That is the limited "courtesy" they extended to me because, in that moment, they defied all the policies and rules that ministries like the MCFD and CPS are supposed to follow. Every child and family services legislative act in each of Canada's provinces and territories states, in some form or another, that children are to automatically go to next of kin. I have no criminal record, don't use drugs, and have no alcohol issues. There was no reason whatsoever that my grandchild shouldn't have gone to me immediately while we sorted this mess out.

But these thoughts came much later. In that instant, I was utterly shattered. I didn't understand why my presence there wasn't being considered "in the child's best interest." My emotions and the room around me were in utter chaos. People were coming and going in and out of the room, and I had no idea who they all were. The foster parents hadn't arrived yet.

I knew my daughter had made some mistakes—who hasn't?— but did it really warrant taking a newborn baby at two weeks? None of this was making any sense, and the stress and confusion were overwhelming. At some point, winky-face Kathy encroached on my daughter's space in the corner and my daughter became very agitated. Winky-face Kathy, perhaps realizing the foster parents were on their way, would have to try to "extract" the baby from her mother's arms. She suggested *I* hold the baby instead.

The only thing that made sense in that chaos was me holding my grandbaby. I looked down at her and was utterly surprised to see her looking up at me. What struck me was the clarity of that instant and how calm this two-week-old infant was, oblivious to the utter chaos going on around us. She was so alert, looking right at me, and her eyes were the most brilliant blue, with a radiance and light shining within them.

Obviously, because it's not possible for words to be articulated from a two-week-old child, I *felt* my granddaughter say to me, *Grammy, it's okay. This (mess) around us, it's temporary. It won't last. You and Mommy are going to get me back because I belong to you and you belong to me. You're my Grammy. Everything is going to be all right.*

It was an instant, yet her "words" will last an eternity. I'd never experienced anything like that before: to have these "words" communicated to me at the lowest point of my life.

Many months later, a Cree elder who I shared this story with didn't even miss a beat. "Tina," she said, "that child's spirit spoke to you."

I have no better explanation than that as to what happened in that moment.

2

IN COURT

---

*D*eplorable is the only word that comes even close to describing what it was like to go into that government MCFD office with our baby and then having to leave without her. I guess I should count myself lucky. Whatever pain and discomfort I'd experienced in my life up until then was just "boot camp." I had to live to be fifty-two years old to experience what real trauma felt like.

I don't know how I was able to operate a motor vehicle, driving back to our hotel. I remember it was raining. I remember automatically knowing to turn on the wipers, but the tears streaming down my face couldn't be so easily swiped away.

When we got back, Suzanne was waiting in the doorway of our hotel room and broke down when she saw we didn't have the child. I walked past her and couldn't deal with it. I climbed into bed and stared at the wall. At some point, I called my husband, but the phone call trailed off as I couldn't keep it together. Grief comes in waves, and as I lay in bed that night, the sobs would ebb and wane.

At some point, I heard Suzanne ask my daughter if I'd eaten. Her training kicked in, and the first thing she did was get freezer bags so my daughter could continue to express her breast milk.

So much of what CPS does is in the grey area of the law, but serious legal arguments can—and should—be made for a mother's right to breastfeed her newborn.

The next thing Suzanne recommended was that we get a journal and start recording everything. She was my daughter's constant companion and support that weekend. I was of no use, and I'm useless now trying to even find the words to describe what my daughter must've been feeling. In fact, I don't think she was feeling at all.

She stared at the TV. She demanded that we get rid of all the baby stuff. The adorable little outfits and diapers that had been so neatly stacked the moment we checked in now had to be stuffed in the trunk of the car. We said very little. In Suzanne's experience, she knew that the chances of getting the baby back were slim. To her credit, she remained silent on this point. We called winky-face Kathy often that weekend to let her know that more breast milk had been expressed and she was to get it to the foster parents. On Sunday afternoon, on one such trade-off time, she made us wait almost half an hour. As I sat in the car, she actually had the audacity to wave at me. I ignored her.

On Monday morning at 9 a.m. sharp, I phoned the MCFD office and got the director, Bee.[5] I demanded to see my grandchild. I knew we had to be afforded some rights in all of this, the least of which were visits. She said to me, "Yes, we're on it."

The foster parents were an older couple and, from what I could register through all this, fairly nice people. I knew that every time we demanded visits, it was they who had to drive into town to the office to comply. I didn't know anything about the pay structure of fostering, and I didn't care. All we had in our life at that point were visits with the baby, and we were going to take whatever we could get.

That first visit was surreal. After the routine "identity stripping" greeting by the receptionist, we were led into a much more casual room, this time with couches and a TV. There was a box

---

[5] *Again, not her real name. Again, perhaps in a second edition.*

filled with his-and-hers toys, and it was clear that it was a family visiting room. My daughter and I sat side by side on the couch and she nursed her baby. My arm rested around my child and we said little. Suzanne warned us that the room was probably bugged, but it was easy not to be worried about that. We soaked up every second of that hour with the baby, and the only noise was her suckling at the breast. I got to hold my grandchild, my gentle patting urging forth a precious little burp.

Every time one of these visits ended, even more of my daughter's heart was ripped out.

After this first visit, we stopped in the lobby on our way out. My daughter needed the bathroom. She didn't want to waste a moment of that hour going to the bathroom. I was still so utterly confused and shocked that we didn't have our baby, and the stress was overwhelming. I couldn't keep from bursting into tears as I waited for my daughter. Behind an opaque glass partition between the lobby and the other rooms we were getting to know, one by one, I caught the shadow of Bee spying on us.

Court was set for the next day. I'm not sure what information she was looking for.

Later that Monday, we received some unexpected advice that proved to be invaluable. News had travelled over the weekend about what we were going through. A young lady—we'll call her "Carla"—knew some people who were friends with my daughter. She had seen a social media post and somehow got our number. Carla had just been through what we were going through. Her baby had been taken by the MCFD three months earlier and she had persevered in getting her daughter back. Long story short (because all these cases are detailed and complicated, essentially all their own books), she said that we have to have the right *attitude* when dealing with the MCFD. "You can't be confrontational with them, even though you feel like smashing their faces in and taking off with your baby," she said. "You have to be meek, indulging the MCFD into thinking you're all on the same page." Meanwhile, the truth is that the MCFD would just be waiting for us to screw up so they can keep the baby. Just keep repeating

"How do we get our baby back?" and follow through with everything the MCFD asks you to do. Do it submissively, letting them think they have the upper hand.

Biting our tongues is not something my daughter and I do well, but we listened to Carla's advice. Essentially, what she was saying is, "Do you want to be right or do you want your baby back?" With the MCFD, you can't have both. You have to let them think they're right and bide your time until they've run out of dirty tricks.

We listened to Carla's advice. We wanted our baby back.

So, unbeknownst to the MCFD, we were ready for the presentation hearing on Tuesday, March 14, 2017. We had to forfeit a precious visit with the baby that day. We'd been getting our paperwork in order, talking to Suzanne and Carla to discuss a united strategy, and arranging for a lawyer. We were trying to gather enough evidence to have the case dismissed and have the judge see it for the joke it was, but that's not what the presentation hearing is for. Apparently, it's just the first step favouring the one-sided vantage of the MCFD's systematic routine of taking babies. Generally, judges just look to see if a "ticky box" is checked off and then it's on to the next case.

Incidentally, the reason given on that horrible Friday afternoon was that my daughter had breached her "safety plan" by staying at the hotel with me. On the forms presented to the court on Tuesday, the "ticky box" that social workers checked was "unwillingness to care for child" or some such shit like that. Even though everything—and I mean *everything*—we were doing was negating that lie, judges usually just see what the social workers put in front of them on paper. MCFD is well versed and practised in knowing court procedures. In fact, we had a letter from my daughter's doctor recommending that the baby be returned to her mother, but I'm sure the judge was not shown that letter either.

We lucked out with a good lawyer, though, and were digging in for a fight. I'll just share his first name, which is Dan. (He died a couple of years after our case, so I would prefer to protect the privacy of his family.) I wondered if winky-face Kathy was starting to realize that perhaps they'd made a mistake in taking our baby. But I knew the MCFD would never admit that.

Something happened during the night after the presentation hearing with regard to the baby's father. He had a right to be there, of course, and the MCFD had a legal obligation to notify him of his daughter being in the custody of the province. The MCFD had a legal obligation to notify him of the date of the presentation hearing. He and my daughter were not together as a married or common-law couple, but my daughter did want him to know his child. She just didn't want his lifestyle, and her priority was to provide the best life she could for Bianca.[6]

Instead of showing up for court that Tuesday, he reached for drugs that night. They were laced with fentanyl, and what happened to him is what's been happening to so many young people these days.

He died.

Just like that, his life had changed and ended. He had a daughter taken by the MCFD at two weeks old. By the time she was a month old, his funeral had come and gone. Winky-face Kathy didn't know what he'd done on the night of the presentation hearing when she scheduled a meeting with us on Thursday, March 16. She had a list of things to discuss. Before going through her list, she needed us to state exactly what we wanted, for the record.

My daughter and I looked at each other, confused, and then looked back at winky-face Kathy, stating the obvious: "We want our baby back."

This time, I didn't record the meeting. We had Dan with us because we had immediately told him the news about the baby's father. He made a point of being there with us, though he let us do all the talking.

---

[6] At my daughter's request, I've changed the name of my grandchild.

When winky-face Kathy came to the issue of the baby's father on her list, again my daughter and I looked at each other. *She didn't know.*

I didn't elaborate on what had happened and simply stated, "He died." Winky-face Kathy was visibly surprised. She wriggled in her seat, freed her arms from her side, and leaned just a smidgen toward my daughter. Good grief! Was she actually going to hug my daughter?

"Please don't touch her," I said firmly yet politely.

I swear she had to sit on her hands for the rest of that meeting to prevent any further theatrics.

The next few weeks after that meeting were a blur. Each day, visits with our baby had to be cleared by MCFD and coordinated with the foster parents. Day after day, these visits reinforced our commitment to having baby and mother reunited (and reinforced my presence as grandmother to my grandchild and advocate to my daughter). Our discussions with winky-face Kathy would've been more confusing if we hadn't kept remembering Carla's advice to "always bring the conversation around to 'What do we have to do to be reunited with our baby?'"

I don't know if MCFD noticed us asserting our rights as much as possible, but these discussions were leaning toward me agreeing to temporary custody of my grandchild with a simultaneous supervision order over my daughter.

I was okay with that.

What I wasn't okay with was MCFD's further inconsistent and confusing actions. My daughter was practically cowering anytime they came into the room. She was dejected and miserable, and I could see it in her body. And during one of our visits with Bianca, winky-face Kathy tempted my daughter by saying, "We could give custody back to mother," which got my daughter to sit straight up.

I was incredulous!

Not two weeks earlier, the baby had been taken because "mother was unwilling to care for her," or some such BS. All of the sudden, she's good to go with having custody again? I saw it for what it was. A trap. I instructed my daughter to think this through.

MCFD would pretend everything was good until I returned home. Then they went back to square one, setting up my daughter's failure using other tactics.

I turned to winky-face Kathy and said, "No. The only custody we'll discuss is *joint-custody*." And I followed up this latest development with a phone call to our lawyer (Dan), while she was still next to me.

This roller-coaster ride, of first taking the baby and then verbally suggesting they give her back, all happened within the time span of a few weeks in March 2017. In April, MCFD had no choice but to follow their own policies and let me appear in court to be granted an interim order, so I could collect my family and get them back home where we all belonged. They continued putting obstacles in our path to reunification, constantly harping that it was "in the best interest of the child."

I needed to do what I'd originally come to this shithole town to do: help my daughter get set up in a new place to get a fresh start as a mother. We accomplished that, but it came at great expense to me. I had to drain my savings, which wasn't much but it was all I had, and then it was gone.

Fortunately, it was just enough to prevent them from dragging things out in court by turning months into years, and to get them out of our lives. The three-month supervision and custody orders were stressful but not nearly as stressful as having the baby in foster care and having to coordinate visits. The MCFD still tried their tactics, but it was difficult for them to gain the upper hand. We were in a different province, so they were quite limited in what they could "dig up." Sometime in June 2017, they sent even more forms for me to sign to get kinship care funding. I read through the forms and didn't like what I saw. I refused to sign. After a month of applying as much pressure as they could from a distance, they realized I wasn't going to sign. It was July 2017. They were done. But they kept trying to find an angle just the same.

After the three-month supervision and custody orders were up in August 2017, another court date had to be scheduled. We knew everything was fine. Dan, our lawyer, knew everything was fine. Yet the MCFD turned around and wanted to extend the same court orders for another three months, essentially dragging things out until November 2017. They had no other "play" in their playbook. We were notified, as usual, in late afternoon on Friday on an August long weekend. Court would be in five days' time on the following Wednesday. We couldn't get ahold of Dan until Tuesday. I left him countless messages, packing our bags with one hand and hitting redial with the other. He called back to say he would stand in our stead the following day in court.

We didn't need to state the obvious: "Oppose any further measures."

Opposing a three-month extension meant another court date was set a month later, in September 2017. This time, we were ready for their antics, and this time my husband came with us. He had some contract work to fulfill the summer of 2017, but by September his work was done. My husband drove and it was a beautiful day. On my drive there, seven months earlier, I was alone and had barely noticed the majestic Rocky Mountain scenery. This time, we enjoyed their beauty and talked, still a little more anxious about this court date but far better prepared for the foe we were up against.

During the summer of 2017, we had met a dad taking his paternity leave. His wife was a very busy lawyer, so he was being a house dad while his second child was still just a few months old. We'd met him in a parenting group, with our babies about the same age. He invited us to their home, so we got to meet his busy wife. I will never forget the advice she gave me. And since she's a lawyer, it was pro bono and out of the kindness of her heart. She had witnessed the antics of social workers more times than she could count, and her advice ended up being quite relevant to us on that September day when our name was called in court.

"Tina, when you're called in court, take the baby with you," she said. "Don't ask for permission. Just do it. Sit at the very front so the judge sees the child."

And that's exactly what we did. My daughter and I walked in first, followed by my husband carrying Bianca. I swear, out of the corner of my eye, I saw the bailiff's jaw drop, but I didn't care. Earlier that morning, when winky-face Kathy saw us waiting in the courthouse gallery, she'd whispered to her co-worker and they both looked up at us. Now, I know my daughter well enough to know it probably took every ounce of discipline for her not to flip them the bird.

I wasn't there for a congeniality contest either. My daughter had been through enough, and we needed to put a stop to the MCFD.

In a series of lucky stars we'd had the good fortune to gaze upon during the past seven months, two of those stars were in the courtroom that day: our lawyer, Dan, and that judge. He started to do what any person with common sense should've done seven months earlier: he started asking questions. He questioned the need to go to trial over "this." He questioned if there were other means by which the MCFD could see this resolved. And he questioned whether a resolution could be found that day. Dan explained, while standing at the bar, that we had travelled from Alberta to be there that day. The judge nodded his acknowledgement. Dan later told us that judges would (sometimes) put a priority on a case if they knew the family had made the extra effort and incurred the extra expense to be there, as we just had.

After the judge posed these open-ended questions, we waited outside the courtroom for an available private room. Dan was still busy, and the MCFD's lawyer had the audacity to walk right past me and my husband and try to speak to my daughter privately before this meeting. I have never been more proud of my daughter's learning curve from the past few months. She told him, very politely, that we would wait for Dan.

In that tiny room, after months of the MCFD dragging their heels and intentionally perpetuating stress and confusion, we finally got a resolution to this nonsense and an end in sight. It was like some sick poker game. Winky-face Kathy said she wanted another two months added to the orders. My husband said, "No way." At least she knew not to ask for three months, as the judge had just started questioning things. But she didn't like that we weren't accepting two months either. She said had to call her supervisor.

So, I thought, *start dialing.* I don't know if it ever registered in their pea brains that this was all being done because of a baby. She and the lawyer left the room to make the call.

Dan, my husband, my daughter, and I all had a chance to talk in private. The longest we would go was one more month. We waited for them to return.

Winky-face Kathy continued to be vague, wanting to see "more stability" on the part of my daughter and wanting to continue to have Alberta social services look in on us. She went on and on, speaking without actually saying anything. And then she directed a comment to me, bringing up this form for "funding" that I had never signed. I turned to Dan and asked, "Why do I have to listen to this? This isn't a trial!"

I don't know if it was my incredible sense of frustration that diffused any further pussyfooting around, but we all walked out of that room in agreement. One more month and it would be over. When I reflect on that final meeting with winky-face Kathy, my chatty daughter did very little speaking. She sat in the corner, with her baby sleeping on her lap, while my husband and I did most of the negotiations. We had grown together as a family, and we had won.

Instead of the usual rubber-stamping judges do to side with whatever social workers say, His Honour that day put a one-month expiration date on our case, and that was the end of the MCFD for us. I wanted to kiss his feet.

Relief doesn't even come close to describing the feeling when we left court that day. It must've been around two, maybe closer to three o'clock, and we'd been waiting at the courthouse since it opened at 8:30 a.m. We were starving.

We stopped for fast food before the long drive home and, as we all sat down to eat, my daughter was the first to comment on the day's events. "When I saw the look on Kathy's face," she said, "it was well worth the trip."

It was the first laugh we'd had in months.

3

FANCY PRISON

A few weeks after that last court date—sometime in late September 2017—I sent a very heated letter to the then-minister of the MCFD.[7] It had been cathartic for me to write my day-to-day feelings in our temporary home while serving out the three-month temporary custody and supervision orders.

My daughter refers to that time as "fancy prison."

And that collective laugh we had shared as a family on the last court date would be the beginning of our healing and the first of many laughs to come. I know our ability to maintain a sense of humour—albeit dark at times—kept us going during those months in isolation. We honestly didn't know if Bee, the director who hid behind that opaque partition, had sent "minions" to Alberta to spy on us, so we kept to ourselves and basked in the joy of having our baby with us.

My daughter and I are human, though, and we got on each other's nerves.

It was extremely humiliating for her to be forced to live with her mother and be treated like she was a danger to her own

---

[7] *In the four years since our ordeal, there have been three ministerial changes in that position.*

child. I didn't treat her that way, and there had never been any doubt in my mind that I was doing the right thing, helping my daughter get through these ridiculous court orders and get the MCFD out of our lives. But the court orders had to be followed, and I was not to leave my daughter alone with her own child.

Alberta social services checked in on us several times, starting in April 2017 through to September 2017. They saw no protective concerns, and we weren't too worried about them. They were already proving to be more reasonable to deal with than British Columbia. I think their director could see a traumatized grandma and mother with a shared love of their baby. All that was needed was time.

Hence, our "sentence" in fancy prison.

We made the best of it. Despite our shell-shocked state, my daughter and I had reconnected and talked through the wake of the confusion we'd experienced. She started to settle into our new home far better than I did. I was away from my husband, but it was temporary. My daughter had her baby to care for, and she could start making up for lost time. She cooked and cleaned. She started to gain some weight, and so did the baby. Each day that passed, the shock of what we'd just gone through started to wear off a little more, and our love for Bianca solidified.

Because I couldn't work and essentially had to just be there "supervising," I started to pore over every piece of paper that the MCFD had thrown at my daughter. Most of the court documents were redundant. The MCFD would first apply to the courts regarding Bianca's custody; then the application would be rubber-stamped by the judge, and a court order would ensue.

It was infuriating reading the MCFD's narrative in these pages. The sheer volume of this documentation was one thing, but the blatant embellishment of turning marijuana into "meth addiction" was quite another. It simply is not true. Cannabis is not methamphetamine.

I would like to set the record straight here, though, because my daughter has made mistakes. In her late teens, she met a guy just as she was graduating high school. I didn't particularly like him, but I hadn't chosen my daughter's friends for her growing up, so I wasn't about to start then. I knew she was making a mistake with him. She tried to make the relationship work for six years and, during that time with him, didn't get pregnant despite not being on the pill. When the relationship fizzled, as I knew it would, my daughter partied like a rock star. Getting pregnant wasn't a concern because, in the back of her mind, she may have thought she couldn't get pregnant. I've asked her if she thought that, but my daughter says she doesn't remember. That time after she broke up with him was a blur, and she remembers being rather lost in life.

Like I said, she's not perfect. She certainly isn't the first young woman to choose a mate her mother didn't approve of, and I'm certain she won't be the last. When my daughter realized she *had* gotten pregnant right away with someone else, she stopped partying. The MCFD's narrative had her continuing to party and added "meth" to the list of drugs they had presented to the courts. It just wasn't true, but it didn't seem to matter. We got hauled into court just the same.

By the time our last court date had arrived in September 2017, I'd had to listen to the MCFD's embellishments of my daughter's shortcomings five times.

The first time was at the presentation hearing in March 2017. Setting parents up to fail and preparing the paperwork for court is all part of the MCFD's routine. Winky-face Kathy had handed Dan the documents and, later, it was a sickening list of drugs for a mother to have to read. My daughter became furious at the MCFD's embellishments when she, Suzanne, and I had had time to read and reread these documents later at the hotel.

The second time I had to listen to this same character assassination of my daughter was in April 2017, when the courts agreed to an interim order while I gathered my baby girls and moved us all back to Alberta, where we belonged.

The third time was in May 2017, when I signed the temporary three-month custody and supervision orders.

The fourth time was in August, when Dan relayed to me what had been repeated by winky-face Kathy in court. He didn't understand why they were just saying the same thing over and over again, without any acknowledgement or concession as to how well my daughter was adjusting to motherhood.

The fifth time was when I had returned with my family, including seven-month-old Bianca, to face the MCFD in court in September 2017. I had to listen to winky-face Kathy assassinate my daughter's character again. It took all my self-discipline not to lunge across the courtroom and gouge out her eyes.

We had had enough.

This must've all started with a call to the MCFD that my daughter was a "meth head," which wasn't even true. The MCFD chose to ignore the evidence and refused to exonerate her (I'll address this in the next chapter). At each of these five court procedures that I listed, the MCFD just systematically inserted "their reasons" for keeping the child. It's a one-size-fits-all routine, and it is a vile and cruel way to treat human beings.

It's BS.

But we were lucky. We had Suzanne coach us every step of the way. She knew every trick they had up their sleeve and what "reasons" would systematically be injected at certain points in their playbook.

During our sentence in fancy prison, Suzanne came to visit us in July 2017. I don't recall if that summer was when Suzanne told us that she never thought we'd ever get Bianca back, but I remember that she joined me in going over the paperwork with a fine-toothed comb. Remember, Suzanne has had years of experience dealing with this system, so much of the bureaucracy and paperwork I was studying was stuff she'd learned long before.

We talked about my daughter's urine tests, which the MCFD accessed by pressuring her to sign "release of medical information" forms. Suzanne suspected that they had gotten the samples from the doctor's routine test of pH levels during pregnancy. We talked about accessing information that wasn't in all the documentation I was poring over. In order to do that, we'd have to apply to get all the social workers' notes and paperwork that wasn't filed in court through the Freedom of Information and Protection of Privacy Act (FOIPPA).[8] Suzanne coached us through that, too, as there's a specific way to word the application for the best outcome.

At this point, I'd like to acknowledge that not once, during any of the court dates, were we able to present any paperwork or "evidence" to support our side of the case. All the judge was seeing was what the MCFD was filing in court. During that summer, we collected paperwork to support our case if we ever got some form of evidentiary hearing. It seems that no such hearing exists, at least not in matters of MCFD/CPS apprehending children. Still, we collected letters of character reference and other paperwork to support my daughter. We kept Bianca's baptismal certificate and a note from our reverend as to our weekly attendance at church. My daughter took it upon herself to have drug tests done for cocaine, pot, meth, crack, etc. Her results were always clean, right across the board.

I kept this file organized as the amount of paperwork supporting my daughter's cause grew. She was busy caring for her infant. The laundry was nonstop as my daughter sorted through outfits that Bianca quickly outgrew.

I forgot to mention that on the morning of the presentation hearing—four days after they'd taken Bianca—Suzanne, my daughter, and I went to the hospital where Bianca had been born. I honestly think the MCFD figured we'd be pushovers in this custody battle. For whatever reason, they'd not had the foresight to alert the hospital. We walked out of the hospital with the nurses' and doctors' notes surrounding Bianca's birth. Suzanne was able to interpret their content for us, as she'd attended countless births as a doula.

The medical information and measurements of the umbilical cord were of particular interest to us—and to the MCFD.

---

[8] *The Freedom of Information and Protection of Privacy Act (FOIPPA) is a right that citizens have to request the government's notes on their case. Generally, in Canada, FOIPPA jurisdictions fall under provincial legislation.*

They'd used a sample of the umbilical cord to further test for drug use in my daughter. The results came back quickly during their "investigation" and they were clean.

After Suzanne returned to her home from that summer visit with us, I looked at the mountain of documents from a different perspective. I started to see a pattern in the MCFD's systematic routine of exploiting poor parents using the court's procedural timeline. It starts with a phone call from somebody with "a crystal ball of good intentions." Someone had thought my daughter would be a shitty mother. They were wrong. The MCFD was wrong. Whereas this "Good Samaritan busybody" is just someone who needs to get a life, the MCFD social workers are paid by tax dollars and they have a duty to be professional and objective, especially with matters involving children. Instead, they inserted themselves into my daughter's life, her pregnancy, and even that special moment when a new mother meets her baby for the first time. They do this using an insidious tool known as birth alerts.

Birth alerts are starting to receive much criticism in the news in Canada, as they should. Basically, the system is some kind of "pseudo red flag" with which social workers place a label on expectant mothers they consider to be high-risk. These expectant moms or dads are flagged for various reasons. For example, if one of the expectant parents has grown up in the child welfare system, they're invariably deemed high-risk. A birth alert is attached to their "file" and the MCFD and CPS are notified as soon as they arrive at the hospital in labour.

The expectant parents are usually unaware of this "red flag" and check into the hospital excited to welcome their newborn into the world. Instead, their lives are turned upside down when a social worker appears and literally scoops up the baby, sometimes just a few hours old. As I said, birth alerts are starting to gain some traction in the news under the Personal Health Information Protection Act (PHIPA) under Canadian charter law.

I will touch on the "lack of mainstream media" later in the book. For now, I will just emphasize that we experienced this same attitude of secrecy and were blindsided by the actions of MCFD social workers.

In the years that have passed since our ordeal, there is one particular thing that has really bugged me. MCFD social workers were able to order all these tests on my daughter. During the last month of my daughter's pregnancy and two weeks prior to Bianca's apprehension, the MCFD got access to my daughter's urine, as well as the umbilical cord. When I arrived in town, they may or may not have already been in the process of having the placenta sent away for testing, and I'm calling BS on this. The system is rigged. The MCFD is able to order these tests be done to prove their side of the case. But us? We had to wait over a year until our file was closed. We had to go through the process of applying through FOIPPA to get our paperwork and then were denied access to the tests done on my daughter's placenta. This is a perfect example of how one-sided the system is, rigged to set parents up to fail, and how woefully lacking it is in answers and justice for families that have been wronged.

4

HUMANS, AKA LAB RATS

More than a few times during our ordeal, I would give my head a shake and wonder, *How is any of this legal?* The MCFD's actions were so foreign to me, and it is a credit to my best parenting efforts. I had never experienced "the system" like this before, and the harder we tried to make sense of what the MCFD was doing, the further from logic and reason we found ourselves.

One of the questions I've been asked a lot these past few years is, "If you hadn't been there for your daughter, what would've happened?"

On the day of the presentation hearing, four days after Bianca was taken, I was waiting in the court gallery. This courthouse was designed much like any, I suppose. I think it had two main court-rooms: one in addition to the one we always seemed to be in. Then there were various hallways and recesses in the walls from the main gallery and corridor outside the courtrooms. One of these probably led to the judge's chambers. There was a thick glass wall separating the corridor and gallery that descended to the main staircase.

I was behind the thick wall of glass, standing in the gallery where some of the waiting people sat. Behind me was another glass wall into other government offices, and there were bathrooms, duty counsel offices, and an elevator at the top of a main winding staircase.

Despite being behind the thick glass wall, I heard the most gut-wrenching howl escape from one of the hallways. It was loud, and I cringe now remembering it and the pain behind it. Other curious people, waiting for their turn in court, gravitated toward the sound of this anguish, trying to get a glimpse of its source.

I was disgusted. I remained where I was, thinking only one thing: *I bet that parent just discovered they'd been tricked into signing a CCO.*[9]

I bet some lawyer was explaining it to that poor parent, and the ramifications of it will shatter their life forever. The lawyer would've said something like, "It means 'continuing custody order.' It means you cannot see your child again. No visits. No contact. Your child is now in the permanent custody of the government." It sounded like the guttural howl of a mother in labour, but I couldn't be sure it wasn't a man's voice either.

From the moment the MCFD announced that they were taking Bianca, my daughter let out her own war cry and was prepared to fight. She did get ahold of a lawyer in the flurry of phone calls she made as she instinctively grabbed her baby and tried to get away from the social workers. What this lawyer said on the phone was that he was too busy and couldn't take on any more clients. He then proceeded to explain what my daughter's next steps should be.

She doesn't remember the steps the lawyer described at all.

It would be akin to a driving instructor having the day's lesson be about the importance of the "ten and two" positioning of the hands on the steering wheel while the car hit a patch of ice and slid out of control toward the edge of a cliff. My daughter was in shock and couldn't register what this lawyer was telling her on the phone.

---

[9]   *Continuing custody order.*

All of this paperwork gets dumped onto parents when they are in a state of shock, confusion, and anger as their child is being taken. Yet, ministries like the MCFD and CPS actually think it's *reasonable* to expect poor parents in this state to mount a proper legal defence and sort through this mountain of documentation in a matter of a few days. Most CPS policies state, in some form or another, that parents have the right to a court date within days of their child being taken. In British Columbia, it is within seven days. Social workers who are skilled at knowing what to present in front of a judge can exploit these tight timelines. Parents cannot. My daughter needed—and had—a team helping her: Dan, our lawyer, obtained through legal aid; Suzanne and her vital knowledge of the operations of the MCFD; and me, who had next-of-kin legal rights to my granddaughter.

Most parents don't have these resources and certainly could never pursue it to the extent that we have over the past four years. I wanted Dan to sue the MCFD on our behalf. He died. I went looking for another lawyer and finally found one with offices in my hometown in Ontario. Rogerson Law Group spent many months being brought up to speed on what had happened in our case. After all this back and forth, which took many months and ate up my retainer, I realized, in the summer of 2020, that the statute of limitations was up on us being able to sue. In British Columbia, the statute is two years, which isn't very long. Though Rogerson Law Group wasn't able to help us with a lawsuit, they did answer some legal "hairsplitting" questions I had and did so pro bono before the year 2020 ended.

Here are the findings of their report in response to my questions about the MCFD taking my daughter's placenta samples:

December 2020
Rogerson Law Group
Toronto, Canada

The client is in the process of writing a book that outlines the problems they had with the MCFD with the removal of a baby from the custody and care of her mother shortly after birth. The client is the grandmother of the baby and on its face will not be entitled to the same disclosure rights afforded to the birth mother. The mother and grandmother had a good relationship during this ordeal, and their interests were always aligned in their dispute with the MCFD. The mother was never a client of Rogerson Law Group (RLG).

The issue the client had is with social workers being allowed to test her daughter's placenta specifically looking for evidence. The client says that the birth mother was never able to get access to those same test results and, therefore, not allowed to present their lack of findings as evidence to support a dismissal of the MCFD's case to apprehend the baby.

Client states: "In 2017, my grandbaby was taken by CPS social workers when the baby was two weeks old. Part of their 'investigation' was taking placenta samples right after birth and sending them to a lab. We never got the results, but we know the results came back clean because there was no reason to be looking for something that wasn't there. That didn't stop CPS, as they continued to drag things out unnecessarily in court for months. Can a lack of evidence not be used as evidence to apply to courts to have the case dismissed and litigation disrupted?"

RLG: What is the placenta?

The placenta is a structure that develops in the uterus during pregnancy. In most pregnancies, the placenta is located at the top or side of the uterus. In placenta previa, the placenta is located low in the uterus.

Source: Mayo Clinic

What does placenta testing reveal?
* *Preferred process for collection is at birth for all infants; test immediately for high-risk births, store for low-risk births*
* *Collection based on need (e.g., history of drug exposure, maternal urine screen results)*

- *Fastest, most sensitive, and definitive testing when positive results are expected for cannabis use, heroin use, fentanyl, etc.*
- *Umbilical cord testing is thought to reflect maternal drug use during approximately the last trimester of a full-term birth; tests to detect marijuana and alcohol are available separately from the panel*

Source: Gwendolyn A. McMillin, PhD, Professor of Clinical Pathology, University of Utah, Scientific Director, Mass Spectrometry Platform; Medical Director, Clinical Toxicology and Pharmacogenomics, ARUP Laboratories

(It is interesting to note that social workers created a situation where they used "impending lab results" to try to plant fear and doubt in my mind. The reason lab results were "impending" is that the placenta had to be sent to the United States. The MCFD had already tested my daughter's urine. Clean. They kept digging and tested the umbilical cord. Clean again. Shouldn't that, plus my daughter's words "I don't use meth—never have, never will," be enough? Because then it was the placenta MCFD sent away to be tested at what is starting to add up expense after expense, courtesy of the B.C. taxpayer. How long should the MCFD be allowed to embark on this "fishing expedition" and how invasive into a human being's body should they be allowed to be?)

RLG goes on to ask …

What is the Ministry of Child and Family Development?

The Ministry of Child and Family Development's primary focus is to support all children and youth in British Columbia to live in safe, healthy, and nurturing families and be strongly connected to their communities and culture. It is also responsible for developing universal, affordable, accessible, quality, and inclusive childcare. The ministry's approach is to provide inclusive, culturally respectful, responsive, and accessible services that support the well-being of children, youth and families in British Columbia.

Source: Government of British Columbia

What is the legislation that governs the MCFD?

Part 3 governs child protection and provides the MCFD with its power to be used in accordance with the best interest of the child.

Division 7: Procedure and Evidence
Full disclosure to parties

64 (1) If requested, a party to a proceeding under this Part, including a director, must disclose fully and in a timely manner to another party to the proceeding

(a) the orders the party intends to request

(b) the reasons for requesting those orders

*(c) **the party's intended evidence***

(2) The duty to disclose under subsection (1) is subject to any claim of privilege

(3) Evidence may be excluded from a hearing under this Part if no reasonable effort was made to disclose the evidence in accordance with this section.

Me to RLG: After our file was closed, around the time the baby turned one year old, we applied to the Freedom of Information and Protection of Privacy Act (FOIPPA) to get these lab results and were denied access as we were not able to prove how these results would be "in the best interest of the child." It's ridiculous. My legal question is, shouldn't these lab results have been made available to both parties early on in our case and, finding no evidence to back up allegations that my daughter was a "meth head," shouldn't we at least have been afforded the legal argument to apply to have her case dismissed and the baby returned immediately? In other words, shouldn't we have been afforded the courtesy of "innocent until proven guilty" and been able to use their lack of evidence as evidence supporting reunification of mother and baby?

RLG: Canadian Charter of Rights and Freedoms

1. *The Canadian Charter of Rights and Freedoms guarantees the rights and freedoms set out in it subject only to such*

reasonable limits *prescribed by law as can be demonstrably justified in a free and democratic society.*

Proceedings in criminal and penal matters

11. Any person charged with an offense has the right:

1. To be informed without unreasonable delay of the specific offense

2. To be tried within a reasonable time

3. Not to be compelled to be a witness in proceedings against that person in respect of the offense

4. To be presumed innocent until proven guilty according to law in a fair and public hearing by an independent and impartial tribunal ...

(I don't think I've spoken to a single parent during and since our ordeal who doesn't say this: they were treated as if they were guilty and had to prove their innocence. This is the closest I can come to explain—certainly not justify or understand the MCFD's actions—that it's because parents are never formally charged under the Criminal Code in child protection cases. Criminals are afforded more rights than parents caught in the web of child protection, and that is why social workers operate in the grey areas of the law. Family court is for civil litigation. It has become the "go to" in acrimonious divorces when "I'll see you in court" is often threatened by immature parents who can't resolve their differences like grown-ups. Ministries like the MCFD have figured out how to exploit marital discord and prop up a multi-billion-dollar industry through their subjective interpretation of what's in the best interest of the child.)

Application of Charter.

32 (1) This Charter applies

1. To the Parliament and government of Canada in respect of all matters within the authority of Parliament including all matters relating to the Yukon Territory and Northwest Territories; and

2. To the legislature and government of each province in respect of all matters within the authority of the legislature of each province

Personal Information Protection Act (PIPA)

2. The purpose of this Act is to govern the collection, use, and disclosure of personal information by organizations in a manner that recognizes both the right of the individuals to protect their personal information and the need of organizations to collect, use, or disclose personal information for purposes that a reasonable person would consider appropriate in the circumstances.

PIPA applies to a doctor's office and a society, among other things.

Source: Guide to B.C.'s Personal Information Protection Act, 2015

PIPA also gives individuals the right to access the personal information an organization has about them and ask for their personal information to be corrected if they think it is wrong or incomplete.

Personal information in court documents or documents created by judges and the courts are not covered by PIPA (section 3(2)e). The same applies to documents containing personal information relating to a prosecution if those proceedings have not completed (section 3(2)h).

Source: A Guide to B.C.'s Personal Information Protection Act

Conclusion

There are several competing laws that govern the disclosure of personal information. Personal information in court documents or documents created by judges and the courts are not covered by PIPA (3(2)e). In this case, a court document created by a judge is what allowed the MCFD to assess the mother's placenta for traces of illicit substances. Because the information in the mother's placenta was not used at any hearing, it was never disclosed by the MCFD. In Canada, the MCFD arguably is not obliged to hand over information they obtained that they did not tender as evidence in the child removal application. Therefore, it becomes more of an ethical question on whether the law should provide for a mandatory disclosure of the birth parent's personal health information of the rightful birth parent despite not using the information as evidence.

Since the MCFD never tendered the test results as evidence in the proceedings for child protection, it became evident to the client that the tests were negative. Why did the MCFD not disclose this information to the client when they became aware? The short answer is that there is no legislation that tells them to do so. We still don't know the answer as to whether the tests came back negative, positive, or inconclusive. As a person whose rights are governed by the Canadian Charter of Rights and Freedoms, the mother should be afforded the courtesy of disclosure of the results.

Under the Child and Family Community Service Act, division 7, s. 64, the society does not have to disclose the information unless they intend to use it. In this case, they did not use it.

However, under the Charter, a person is afforded the most basic rights and freedoms to protect against overreaching legislature and decisions made by the government and its agencies. In this case, part of a person's own body was examined and the evidence was basically put aside and discarded without providing the examined individual the results of the test. This is no better than testing a lab rat and not informing the rat of the results. Humans deserve respect and fairness, which is enshrined in the Canadian Charter of Rights and Freedoms. The British Columbia legislature needs to afford more protections that are enshrined within the criminal law provisions of the Canadian Charter of Rights and Freedoms to families involved in child protection proceedings, especially the parents involved. Courts have correctly made their decisions with the best interest of the child as their top concern. However, this should not come at the expense of disclosure obligations within a medical context at the hearing, especially in light of the fact that Ms. Fumo and her daughter were not afforded disclosure and it cost them lost time with their baby and a great deal of expense to fight this application.

This report, which Rogerson Law Group prepared pro bono, was the closest we'd ever get to some sort of lawsuit or legal "justice" after the many issues we'd faced dealing with the MCFD. The statute of limitations in British Columbia to sue the MCFD is two years. Bianca is four years old now, her first year having been consumed by terror and confusion created by the government body. It is very easy for the MCFD to piss away months, which turn into years, both in family court and the aftermath of parents being in a position to sue.

And an apology!? The Canadian government seems to always be about apologies. It isn't worth a tin of beans to us.

When the stakes are the lives of innocent children, clarity is a must to cut through the BS. From the very beginning, parents need to be clearly told what the "charges" are against them so that they can take measurable steps toward being reunited with their children. I didn't understand why, from the very first hearing, the judge didn't ask more questions or want to at least see more "evidence" by the MCFD to validate their reasons for taking the baby. It boggles my mind that so much confusion is allowed to be perpetuated in a court of law when some simple, concrete steps early on can go a long way to alleviating so much stress and heartache.

What's the original complaint? Where's the report on the investigation and assessment done on the parent or parents? Where's the evidence? Why don't judges start asking social workers these questions from day one? These questions can be asked out loud in court so that they go on transcripts and parents can have some clear communication. People have the right to defend themselves and have the right to know what the "charges" are and why they're being dragged into court.

In the end, we were very lucky, as we got Bianca back after just twenty-seven days. We came to know the foster mom and dad, and they were very nice people. I don't think that what they were being told by the MCFD and what they were seeing with their own eyes was adding up. On their last night with Bianca, in April 2017, the foster dad admitted to us that he didn't understand why she'd been taken in the first place. In case I didn't already say this to them, we thank them for taking such good care of our baby. I think they knew she deserved to come back to us, and today they'd be happy to hear that she's a vibrant little girl who loves swimming and ballet.

So, the answer to the question, "What would've happened if I hadn't been there?" is that my daughter would have eventually lost her baby. The MCFD has become very skilled at coercing signatures and confusing, even further, what is already a very sensitive, stressful situation. Eventually, my daughter would've broken and signed something she couldn't undo. But, because she had a team, she could assert her right *not* to sign anything further. She had Suzanne coaching her, and Suzanne knew every document the MCFD would slide in front of her. She had me, her mother, and my husband, her stepfather. She had support and space to learn and grow to become the mom she is today. Bianca will grow up calling my husband "Papa" and Suzanne "Oma," which means *grandmother* in Dutch.

Our World Full of Beautiful Babies

5

OMA

anff is an exquisite little town nestled in the majestic Canadian Rocky Mountains. I'd lived there for thirty years, working and raising my daughter as a single mom. One of Banff's consistent social problems seems to be a lack of affordable housing. I was one of the lucky ones. I found a teeny, tiny house that suited my daughter and me just fine. The rent was somewhat affordable, though the utilities were steep at times, especially in the dead of winter, when the pipes would freeze and we would have no running water.

This housing problem is compounded tenfold if a person working in Banff needs a place to live with their dog. That was how we met Suzanne. She was well known in town by all the families with toddlers, as she worked at the local daycare. Suzanne didn't know me and my daughter well, though she'd heard about us through friends and found out we might be able to make room for her and her great big dog. Havoc was his name.

It was a beautiful spring day when Suzanne arrived to meet us and see our place. I was downstairs in the kitchen, and my daughter, who must've been eight or nine years old at the time, was upstairs in her room. Or so I thought. The inside proper of this house was small, and I suspect, once upon a time, it was someone's weekend cottage. What wasn't small was the gorgeous wraparound veranda. It had two front doors and an outer door with a latch for the veranda. The inner front and back doors had proper locks and deadbolts.

Suzanne knocked on the outer veranda door when she arrived. From the rooftop, where she was perched, my daughter heard the knock, looked over the eaves trough, and called down, "Oh, you must be Suzanne!"

Suzanne smiled. It was the first time my daughter had called out to her, in a rather unorthodox way, but it wouldn't be the last.

Thus began the time of "three gals in a teeny, tiny house with a great big dog." My daughter and I had never had a pet dog before and, at the time, I couldn't afford a car either. Suzanne had this yellow VW bus that she called Sunshine. When I wasn't working, we'd all go for walks on mountain trails, and I came to learn how incredibly well trained Havoc was. He would heel by Suzanne's side and not be distracted by the endless scurrying of squirrels, chipmunks, and other creatures on the trail.

Suzanne had the room downstairs, which served the dual purpose of being my bedroom and mine and my daughter's living room. I shared the larger bedroom upstairs with my daughter when Suzanne moved in with us.

Suzanne came to learn how it was that my daughter was on the roof that first day. The window from the upstairs room opened out onto the roof. My daughter could climb out of it. I couldn't. In the winter, if we had a dumping of snow, she and the other kids from the neighbourhood would run through the house and up the stairs. They would clamber out onto the roof and jump, using heaps of snow—deep enough to bury a car—to soften their landing.

Suzanne lived with us for a short time. She was more reserved back then, and I think it was because she'd lost the love of her life in a terrible accident. He'd worked for one of the railroads and was killed instantly when a train he was on exploded. Suzanne spent the rest of her twenties grieving this loss. As she entered her thirties, still single, her biological clock was ticking. Perhaps the time spent with us gave her even more of a desire to have children. I didn't know then, but I do now. Suzanne says she often remembered my parenting style when it was her turn to start her journey as a mother a few years later.

Her biological son—we'll rename him Daniel—was born on April 1, 1999.

She had married the brother-in-law of a mutual friend, and no sooner was she married than she got divorced. Suzanne had wanted to be a mom more than she wanted to be a wife.

Suzanne loves children. I'd already mentioned that she had worked at the local daycare and, in the years since leaving Banff, she had continued her studies in women, children, and midwifery. She became a certified doula and coached countless pregnant moms as they delivered their precious bundles into the world. She was hired by a government office on Vancouver Island to work with pregnant women who were struggling with addiction. Suzanne worked one-on-one with them and helped facilitate the steps and changes these women needed to stay clean and be better moms when their babies were born. It took time—sometimes a year and a half—but the success rate was undeniable. Most of the moms she had worked with got clean, chose better partners and healthier relationships, and went on to have other babies.

Suzanne was also a foster mom and, by then, had accumulated twenty years of experience helping families and children one way or another. As a foster parent, she sat on the board of an organization called Fostering Early Development, whose name speaks for itself.

This is what she did for a living, and she supported her son and herself as a single mother. Daniel was growing up quickly, as children tend to do, and Suzanne began to yearn for another baby. This time, though, she wouldn't wait for a mate. Suzanne tried to get pregnant through anonymous sperm donations.

Her journey to become a mother for a second time turned into an expensive and frustrating fertility challenge. She suffered one miscarriage after another. After years of heartache, Suzanne started to realize that the only way she might ever have another baby was to adopt one.

By then, Suzanne had moved herself and Daniel to the mainland. They lived in Vancouver, and Suzanne worked as an infant development consultant at a women's centre in the downtown's east end. It is an area with high-risk, street-attached women. She tried to help so many moms, like the mothers she'd previously coached to cleaner lifestyles, but these outcomes would be horribly different. Not a single mother she tried to help through this women's centre ever got her child back.

The MCFD played the dirtiest tricks. It astounded Suzanne. She would question serious discrepancies between the social workers' legislated directives and their actual behaviour. It was illogical and confusing. Children seemed destined to bounce around the foster care system, and many of these parents reached for drugs, unable to cope with the loss of a child to the system.

Then, on September 17, 2009, Suzanne was handed a beautiful newborn baby boy, Derek.[10]

His mom was not a client of Suzanne's, and she had continued to use drugs throughout her pregnancy. She did get to know what a good person Suzanne was, and decided Suzanne would be the best person to care for her baby. Everyone involved—the social workers, Derek's family, and his biological mom—were in agreement. It was in Derek's best interest to go to Suzanne.

Understandably, Suzanne fell in love with the baby and made it very clear to the MCFD that she wanted to adopt Derek. A year later, this same mom became pregnant with another boy and still chose drugs over her babies. Suzanne was given him, too.

We'll call the second newborn boy Theodore, or Teddy for short.

Daniel was around ten years old when Derek and then Teddy became a part of their family. On outings, when Teddy still weighed less than twenty pounds, Daniel would carry him while Suzanne had Derek, who was older and heavier. One of the very

---

[10] *Not his real name.*

few photos Suzanne has of all of her boys is with her and Daniel each holding a child in matching baby carriers.

It took quite an effort to get Teddy to twenty pounds. When he was born, his withdrawal symptoms manifested in a failure to keep anything down. Suzanne tried everything to get nourishment into him, and she had finally succeeded in getting Teddy to gain weight.

Derek's symptoms manifested in severe bouts of screaming. Any parent who has suffered through colic episodes with their child knows how nerve-racking this can be. He would shake uncontrollably while screaming, and Suzanne would hold him to absorb his shaking. This frenzy would sometimes last for hours. Derek would eventually outgrow both his screaming and shaking episodes.

Despite these challenges with her newborn boys, this was the happiest time in her life. She was fulfilled, as Derek and Teddy needed a mother and Daniel was the best big brother. She loved all of them dearly. It was also the busiest Suzanne had ever been in her life. The photo I just mentioned was one of the few she'd had time to take.

She homeschooled Daniel. Suzanne would put Derek and Teddy in the play area and look over Daniel's shoulder as he worked through the curriculum.

Derek and Teddy needed to see their pediatrician often. The doctor started listing off all the developmental markers the boys were not meeting, and Suzanne was very engaged in working with him to get the extra therapy the boys needed. These clinical discussions were very manageable for Suzanne. She had studied this for years. But it meant that she was too busy to wait by the phone for the MCFD to call back about the adoption process. Looking back, she knows she needed to have paid more attention to the bureaucracy, but at what cost? Should paperwork be more important than taking care of children?

The MCFD didn't have jurisdiction over Teddy and Derek's adoption anyway. Suzanne would have done better hiring a lawyer and working with their biological mother to come to some sort of open adoption agreement. I questioned this same conflict of interest in our case, as I speculated that the MCFD was putting "the cart before the horse." They seemed to be actively seeking reasons to take Bianca. Was there a family waiting to adopt? If I had better journalistic chops, I would definitely investigate this.

I would question the MCFD's need to even be involved in these types of cases in the first place. It would have been in Derek and Teddy's best interest to have their biological mother's family involved. Even though the family themselves couldn't care for them, they could collectively make decisions on an open adoption on their behalf. What gives the MCFD the right to make decisions instead of Teddy and Derek's blood relatives?

I would challenge the jurisdiction of these types of cases. The MCFD should not have the power to apprehend children while at the same time having the power to adopt them out, too. It's a conflict of interest—one that doesn't sound like it's "in the best interest of the child." It doesn't take a genius to think this through, yet these are the legislative powers given to the MCFD. Social workers can pick and choose which children they apprehend, not because they're most at risk but because they're more adoptable.

Our fair-haired, blue-eyed Bianca would be at the top of their list.

In her book, *Punished 4 Protecting*, Francesca Amato-Banfield challenges CPS as well. She writes, "It's not hard to get to know people. We (advocates[11]) visit grandparents and parents and see the child in their care. When the child looks healthy, happy, loved, and cared for, it is not difficult to see where they belong. The courts make it difficult because the courts are broken. The entire system is broken. And how does a broken system expect to fix a broken family? They cannot do it."

---

[11] *Francesca Amato-Banfield began advocating for other families who were going through what she went through. Her first step was to sit in courtrooms and take notes to help families organize a strategy to get their children back. This "court watch" advocacy is growing, having already started in the U.K. as a "McKenzie Friend" support advocacy.*

I, too, am calling BS on this vile system. Whenever children are moved, first taken from parents and then moved to temporary foster care. Whenever children are moved even further away,[12] constantly moving to different foster homes. Whenever children get medical "assessments" by doctors bankrolled by the MCFD. Innocent kids can't connect with their families. They're constantly being moved. Different "professionals" keep getting paid every time there's movement. As far as I'm concerned, that's child trafficking. And that's another book—one written by someone else, though. I haven't got the stomach for it.

But I digress. Back to Suzanne. Ultimately, the reason that the MCFD had no jurisdiction to oversee Derek and Teddy's adoption is that the boy's family and cultural ties, by law, supersedes the MCFD's power. But the MCFD led Suzanne to believe otherwise. As it was in our case, the MCFD seems more interested in letting families know they have the *power* to take children instead of the *reasons* they have to do so.

There's a big difference, and that is why the MCFD is so vague in telling parents precisely the reason why they're apprehending their children.

Suzanne's frustration and confusion were mounting, and she was becoming more vocal. She wanted the adoption to go through and, in the meantime, have the boys' therapy sessions paid for by the MCFD so she didn't have to keep dipping into her savings. She was a single mom taking care of four people, including herself, on one income. And she didn't want Derek and Teddy's treatment delayed due to non payment.

So, on her birthday,[13] the MCFD decided to initiate *their* version of a "solution"—their interpretation of what's "in the best interest of the child"—and what happened next is precisely why

---

[12] *One of the MCFD's tactics is to move a baby to a foster family hundreds of kilometres away. It is meant to make visits next to impossible for poor parents, who may have other children at home and may not be able to afford a car.*

[13] *Which, coincidentally, is mine, too. May 15 is also International Day of Families. Ironic, isn't it?*

Suzanne wanted to adopt the boys. She loved them and wanted legal rights as their mother.

On May 15, 2012, social worker Pam Carr showed up on Suzanne's doorstep. Suzanne was inside reading Teddy one of his favourite books. It was a story about bumblebees, and Teddy loved the interactive buttons that made buzzing sounds.

Pam knocked on Suzanne's door. When she opened it, Pam was standing there with another social worker, Debra Watson. They stepped inside and Suzanne had a sinking feeling. She was informed that Derek had already been picked up at his daycare and they would now be taking Teddy.

Suzanne was shattered. She begged the social workers to tell her on what grounds, but they refused to give Suzanne a reason. Pam did most of the talking and just emphasized their power to remove Teddy.

Suzanne insisted that she be given five minutes to pack a few things for the boys. Teddy would surely want to take his favourite bumblebee book, and Derek had a collection of stuffed animals. Every night, he would place his animals in a circle and sleep in the middle of them. And Suzanne remembered his favourite red blanket, too. She packed Teddy's sleeping companion as well. It was one of those cloth toys, with a doll's head, and Teddy would chew on the knots as he fell asleep. Suzanne had toilet-trained Derek by then but not Teddy. He was just two years old, and Suzanne couldn't remember if the social workers gave her extra time to pack his diaper bag.

Blinded by tears, Suzanne begged that she be allowed a few more minutes with Teddy. He clung to her the whole time. Suzanne packed their things with one hand while holding him in her other hand. The MCFD granted Suzanne a few minutes to keep holding Teddy and then, just like that, the MCFD was gone. On her forty-third birthday, the MCFD saw fit to cut Suzanne's family in half.

She later found Daniel hiding in a closet. He could hear voices and had a suspicion about what was going on. He was terrified. He hid because he thought he'd be taken, too.

Sometime later that day or maybe the next—she can't quite remember—Suzanne found the boys' special items in the alley behind her home. In their reckless haste and carelessness, Pam Carr and Debra Watson probably didn't realize they'd dropped these things before whisking Teddy away in the car.

Suzanne, as devastated as she was, clung to hope. She had done right by these boys since they were born. Surely, there was some mistake.

Suzanne was allowed two visits after her sons were taken and a meeting where she hoped to have the reasons for the apprehension clarified. These visits were extremely traumatic for Suzanne and her sons, especially Derek and Teddy. The MCFD had the audacity to manoeuvre to get Daniel alone while Suzanne was distracted with the commotion and emotions of being granted a visit with Derek and Teddy. Daniel recorded the "conversation" and said absolutely nothing to the social workers.

Suzanne raised a smart kid.

But she couldn't get any clarification with regard to Derek and Teddy. Suzanne couldn't understand if she was this supposed danger to her sons, Derek and Teddy, why her biological son could remain with her. She still had rights as Daniel's mother and made that very clear to the MCFD. If they so much as looked at him again or tried to speak to Daniel alone, Suzanne would get a lawyer. The MCFD backed off.

They only know how to operate in the realm of "smoke and mirrors," with their tactics having real-life consequences for families. They prey upon poor families who may not have the money or education to know how to fight, are intimidated by going to court, and are not able to afford a lawyer. The MCFD is only interested in getting parents to sign their forms so they can open a file and start to generate income. Once parents lawyer up, they back off.

Suzanne had the education but not the money.

Besides, it's not a 100 percent guarantee that getting a lawyer will force the MCFD to back off, but it is a calculated "business" guess that they will. At this point, I'd like to challenge your thinking about what a government is supposed to be for its people. Is it to run like a business or is it elected by the people, for the people? Because I don't know if everyone has connected the dots like I had to during all this. The Canadian government is a crown corporation. I'm going to say that again. It's important.

A crown corporation runs like an empire, and the name of the game is profit. It runs like a business, with a balance sheet of income and expenses. The MCFD is a government body and, therefore, a crown corporation. If its priority is to be run like a business, they will not want the cases they've managed to open— with a parent's signature—to cost more than they can potentially earn. The MCFD does not want to pay their own lawyers to fight with the parent's lawyer. But this isn't supposed to be a business; it is supposed to be social services to help families who need help.

Suzanne did lawyer up to try to get Teddy and Derek back. But her lawyer began hitting walls very soon. The social workers stopped taking any calls regarding Suzanne's case. Up until then, a social worker named Jude McLellan had always been on Suzanne's side and wrote glowing assessments, reporting the truth that Suzanne was a wonderful mother. These reports are necessary in any adoption process. After Derek and Teddy were taken, the MCFD replaced Jude with another social worker, thereby inhibiting any further good reports about Suzanne's mothering skills.

The MCFD refused to communicate any information with their lawyer, who, in turn, had nothing new to report when Suzanne's lawyer would press for answers. It is very easy for government bodies like the MCFD to piss away time. Suzanne eventually ran out of money and couldn't pay a lawyer to fight a losing battle.

She had never been able to adopt the boys.

As if taking her sons wasn't enough, the MCFD systematically started to inform everyone connected to Suzanne's life that she had "lost" Teddy and Derek. It's important to note here the distinction between "the boys being taken" and "losing her sons." The former is the truth; the boys "were taken" from Suzanne.

But in the MCFD narrative, the term "losing the boys" is used, and it is assumed that social workers *must have their reasons*. It is the appearance of guilt that is just as destructive as an actual guilty sentence.

The MCFD started with the doctors. Naturally, Daniel had had the same pediatrician as his younger brothers. This doctor wouldn't take any calls from Suzanne anymore and certainly wouldn't book any appointments. She had to look for another family doctor.

Then the MCFD contacted the members on the board of Fostering Early Development. Suzanne had served on this board for years, and her credibility and good work vanished with a phone call.

Suzanne worked with children, so she always needed to have a clean criminal record and vulnerable persons clearance. None of these had been jeopardized because, as I explained in Chapter 4, the MCFD doesn't have the jurisdiction to formally "charge" parents. If they did, parents would be afforded the same rights as people facing criminal charges and have access to legal counsel to defend themselves in court.

The MCFD operates in a grey area, so this campaign to destroy Suzanne's career was all spoken. She took care of other children in her home. Parents in Vancouver were sometimes wait-listed for daycare for years, so Suzanne had no shortage of other children during the day. She had adhered to provincial guidelines and always kept up her first aid and CPR training. Paying for the training to treat adults is more common, but Suzanne maintained both first aid certification and CPR training for children as well. Daycare was the only work she could do after the MCFD destroyed her credibility, and the pay was (and still is) paltry. It didn't take long for Suzanne to run out of money to pay a lawyer to try to get Teddy and Derek back.

To this day, Suzanne still works with children with autism. She still receives funding through the MCFD to work with these children. Nothing is adding up here!?

The last time Suzanne saw Teddy and Derek was August 5, 2013, fourteen months after they'd been taken. Suzanne and their biological mom had stayed in contact, and she knew well enough that when the boys were calling for their mommy, she wasn't the one they meant: it was Suzanne. Even their biological mom, struggling with addiction, had the compassion and where-withal not to deny her children love.

At first, the MCFD facilitated for Teddy and Derek to have unsupervised visits with their biological mom. It's hard to know whether the MCFD knew she was still using drugs. Despite the inconsistency of this, the MCFD's lapse allowed Suzanne to visit with the boys, relying on their biological mother's compassion. For whatever reason, the visits then switched to being supervised. It was reported back to the MCFD that Suzanne was attending these visits.

The MCFD threatened the biological mother that her visits would be taken away if she continued to allow Suzanne to see the boys. They manipulated a vulnerable woman with addiction problems by telling her their narrative and by lying, saying that Suzanne had hurt her sons. That's why Suzanne "lost" them. The MCFD also disclosed how much Suzanne was paid as a foster mother of two boys with special needs. It is extremely under-handed and unethical for the MCFD to share this information and imply that Suzanne had used the biological mom and her boys to line her own pockets. By disclosing this sensitive information to a volatile woman, the MCFD knew they would get exactly the reaction they expected. She threatened Suzanne's life. Suzanne has kept a recording of that threat all these years, in case she winds up dead.

It seems that the tiniest victims of the MCFD's actions are the children. By then, calling Derek and Teddy "tiny" might have been a bit of a stretch. Both her sons had gained an unhealthy amount of weight after they were taken. After everything she went through to finally get Teddy to keep food down, Suzanne had fed them lots of fruits and vegetables and mostly fish for protein.

They were just toddlers when they were taken, and Suzanne could only wonder what they were being fed in foster care.

She cannot even bear to think of that last day. The sadness in Derek's eyes will always haunt Suzanne. She wants her boys to know how loved they were and still are.

Does any of this sound like it's "in the best interest of the child"? Does it sound like it's in Daniel's best interest to witness his mother being destroyed, emotionally and financially? What about his feelings? His rights? Daniel lost two baby brothers, too. What about Teddy and Derek's well-being, losing the only mother they knew as well as their big brother?

Chances are, Teddy and Derek are still bouncing around the foster care system. They were probably moved because the MCFD could easily find someone to take the boys—and the foster funds attached to them—without squawking like Suzanne was. Were their developmental delays ever addressed?

Somehow, Suzanne made her way back to the land of the living. Somehow, because she loved all her boys dearly, she remembered that she still had Daniel. Suzanne had to regain some semblance of her life and carry on.

She never saw her sons again. Today, they'd be approaching their teen years. Teddy would be ten and Derek eleven.

This is the Suzanne my daughter called out to during the second trimester of her pregnancy. She wanted Suzanne there for the birth in a doula capacity. Life truly is amazing sometimes. Suzanne had suffered greatly but gained a tremendous amount of experience dealing with the MCFD. She was there when Bianca was born. She spoke to me on the phone, and the sound of her voice was so reassuring to me the night I became a Grammy.

"Everyone's fine here, Tina," she reassured. "Your daughter's great. It's a girl, and she's beautiful. Everything is beautiful here."

What Suzanne didn't tell me was that the first words out of my daughter's mouth to the nurses who delivered Bianca were, "Don't take my baby."

What Suzanne didn't tell me was that some of the hospital staff were huddled in the corner of the delivery room, uncaring and oblivious to my daughter's pleas. They had received a birth alert red flag attached to this unborn child. Suzanne had overheard them discussing apprehending Bianca immediately and, very loudly, she reminded them, "You can't do that!"

Suzanne knew the Child and Family Services Act inside and out, and it seems that she understood the spirit of the Personal Health Information Protection Act better than the "professionals," too. She was able to get them to back off, for the time being anyway. Twelve days later, I dropped everything in my life and made the trip there, to assert my right to be a grandmother.

It is the smartest thing I've ever done in my life, and I have Suzanne to thank for that.

6

BAR-CODED BABIES

A mother walks into a grocery store. She has her ten-month-old baby with her and looks for a shopping cart that has functional straps to ensure her baby is secure in the cart. She pushes the cart, grocery list in hand, as she begins to navigate the aisles she knows so well.

Everyday scenario, right? Except when the mom gets in line to pay.

She queues up and unloads each item onto the conveyor belt. She glances at the price being rung up each time she hears the "ting." When the grand total is read off to her by the cashier, she sucks in her breath a little. It's more than she expected. As the mom takes mental inventory of how much cash she brought with her, the cashier's gaze becomes sharper. She sees the mom digging through her purse. All of a sudden, the cashier grabs the baby. A bar code appears on the forehead and she scans the child. The bag boy is waiting and whisks the child off to the back room.

The mother, frantic and confused, tries to chase after the bag boy who has her baby but is blocked by the store manager. She still has to pay for her groceries.

Think this is far-fetched? Think again.

The cashier is the social worker, the bag boy represents the police, and the manager is the authorities intertwined in the child's life. Schools, health care, government: they all expect the mom to pay and continue being a contributing member of society despite her distraught state of mind.

In fact, some doctors will now label a mom as "unstable"—due to her grieving over the loss of her baby—and invoice the MCFD for this diagnosis. Barrier after barrier is set up to make it difficult for the mom to get her baby back. Never mind the fact that she now has to find another place to get her groceries. She'll probably have to move because the first thing the MCFD will do is cut off her monthly stipend provided by the government. The child is no longer in her care, so the funds have immediately been redirected to the provincial government. That stipend might have been the difference between eating and not eating. The rest of her modest income goes to rent.

Rent that probably pays for a two-bedroom. Without her baby, the mom has to move into something smaller and cheaper. The MCFD has labelled her a danger to her own child, and the monthly stipend—which governments often pontificate is meant to help alleviate poverty—is withheld.

The MCFD tactics are illogical yet very simple. What they do to this mom is so unbelievable, but that is precisely what happens. No one believes her. She is desperate, turning to every person she can think of to try to help her, but no one does. They assume that the "MCFD must have their reasons," and about that, they are wrong.

Having to move to a small, one-bedroom apartment just reinforces the "poverty" label already slapped on this mom. Now it also becomes the reason—in their fluid, ever-changing litany of reasons—for the MCFD to *not* return the baby to their mother. At this point, members of the foster family, who are strangers to the child, are getting paid more to take care of the child than the mother gets while the MCFD conducts its farce of an "investigation." I'm going to say that again because it's important.

Poverty is often cited on government forms as "an inability to care for the child" and is a reason for apprehension. Yet, when children are placed in provincial care, foster parents are usually paid *more* than if the children had remained with their biological parents.

I'm not even going to elaborate on how ridiculous this is.

Suzanne didn't take in Derek and Teddy for the money. She had been trying to have her own baby but couldn't. I can't think of too many people on this earth who would take in two boys who would surely present so many problems from being exposed to their mother's drugs while in the womb. I could go on and on about the irresponsibility of this woman, constantly choosing drugs over her babies. But the issues of addiction are far beyond my scope. It's best left to professionals who deal with it day in and day out.

Suzanne had had a good relationship with Teddy and Derek's extended family. They, of course, knew the extra attention and work Suzanne was putting in to help the newborn babies wean off of drugs. They supported Suzanne adopting the boys, and if she had just been left alone to continue mothering them, Suzanne would've ensured they knew who their family was. Why would she deny Teddy and Derek love from their biological family? They would have known their aunties, uncles, cousins, and grandparents, and they would have known they were adopted. They would've known their place in the world and how precious and loved they were.

But because the MCFD continued to insert themselves into the situation, the boys lost all of this. Because of the MCFD, the boys just joined the "inferior" rank of other foster kids who are bouncing around the system. Because the MCFD always wants to control the narrative in their version of what's "in the best interest of the child," trips like the following were authorized while the boys were still in Suzanne's day-to-day care. I doubt very much that the MCFD bothers to pay for these anymore.

Social workers travelled with Teddy, Derek, and their biological mom to visit family. None of the aunties nor the grandmother had been able to take the boys in at their birth and care for them as Suzanne had. So, when the MCFD had arranged these trips, it was a waste of time and money. The family supported Suzanne's intended adoption of Derek and Teddy and didn't need the validation. They knew Suzanne wouldn't deny Teddy and Derek their connection to their biological family.

To the tune of thousands and thousands of dollars, courtesy of British Columbia taxpayers, social workers flew themselves, the boys, and their biological mom to a remote community. They stayed in hotels, not with the family. Each of the social workers had their own room. They ate at the hotel for three meals a day. The MCFD had authorized these trips twice instead of paying for the in-home support that Suzanne may have needed, funding the therapeutic services that the boys had needed, or reimbursing Suzanne for the money she was already paying out of her own pocket. This is the MCFD's idea of "in the best interest of the child"!

Was the biological mom's addiction cured during these trips? No. She continued to use and continued to have more babies, all promptly taken at birth and placed into foster care.

Were the boys eventually placed with their biological family? No. They are probably, still to this day, bouncing around the foster care system.

These expenses incurred by the MCFD should be a matter of public record, but Suzanne could never find them. She met wall after wall when she tried to piece together her shattered life after Teddy and Derek were taken. She applied through FOIPPA to get government records on her. The MCFD was never able to clarify why, exactly, her sons were taken. They were never held accountable for destroying Suzanne's credibility with her work peers, her livelihood, or her life. They were careful to ensure that this smear campaign was verbal only, knowing full well that anything documented could be shown in court—just in case Suzanne won the lottery. If she did win the lottery, she could pay for the lawyer to fight for Derek and Teddy and then sue the MCFD in civil court for emotional and financial damages.

These are valid remedies—ones that my husband and I had countless discussions about. Right now, the current funding model that the MCFD seems to be built on focuses on the "more children, more money" concept. It doesn't take a genius to see the conflict of interest here. There is an incentive to apprehend children and put them in provincial custody.

We're certainly not the only ones to question government spending. Seven years ago, a report by British Columbia's Representative for Children and Youth at that time, Mary Ellen Turpel-Lafond, stated that over $66 million had been spent without any functional public policy framework, any meaningful financial or performance accountability, or any actual children receiving additional services because of these expenditures.

Sixty-six million dollars!?

No accountability!?

No discernible difference in the lives of innocent children!?

I am calling BS. If I ran a business or my household like this, there would be serious consequences. I'd be out of business and living on the street in no time. And remember, these ministries are not supposed to be businesses. They're not supposed to run like empires focused on making money. They're supposed to be social services to help those who need help. That's what I want my taxpayer dollars invested in: for children who are most vulnerable in these situations and whose parents need help.

There seems to be no money for prevention or to genuinely help parents if all that's needed is some parental skill development.[14] Winky-face Kathy started pontificating about all the supports in place for my daughter after they'd taken Bianca. Suzanne had thought that perhaps by being there when Bianca was born and having to re-engage with the MCFD once again, she'd finally get some answers as to why Teddy and Derek were taken so long ago.

---

[14] *Reminder: Ministry of Child and Family Development (MCFD) is the same as Child Protection Services (CPS).*

Nada. Zip. No accountability to the taxpaying public.

CPS is a well-oiled moneymaking machine for social workers and all the "professionals" attached to it. In my grocery store scene, taking the baby to the back room would provide jobs for judges, clerks, foster care, lawyers, health care, etc. All are on the government's bankroll—all done "in the best interests of the child" with the utmost of secrecy and an inability to be forthright with parents.

It is a vile system, rife with inconsistencies and conflicts, and certainly not "in the best interests of the child." Authors Maryann Petri and Dr. Eric Keefer compare the machine that is CPS to the Racketeer Influenced and Corrupt Organizations (RICO) Act. The RICO Act is a U.S. federal law that provides for extended criminal penalties and a civil cause of action for acts performed as part of an ongoing criminal organization. These court proceedings are dramatized in *The Godfather* movies.

My husband and I are reasonable people, and we just couldn't understand any of this. In fact, when it came time for me to write this book, I was very specific about using the term "industry" in the subtitle. If you follow the money, you will realize that much of what CPS does is motivated by it. Much to our shock, we heard rumours that MCFD social workers get bonuses every time a newborn baby is apprehended. We wondered if this rumour was true and how much of a bonus was attached to our precious Bianca.

Make no mistake, the power that social workers wield—over which parents get to keep their child and which ones don't—is a subjective narrative that they can spin out in court. It's not objective. They "investigate" how little money and (lack of) resources a parent or parents have. They try to determine how alone or easily isolated each parent can become from their support system (if they even have one) and from each other. They instigate adversity and chaos among the adults in the child's life. Divide and conquer.

The MCFD mostly pontificates about their power to take the child, not their reasons to do so. My daughter and Suzanne were typical targets: poor, single moms. There are a lot of them out there. It is a systematic process, a warehouse of exploited humans, and an industry to keep the child moving and keep the funds flowing. And, apparently, social workers don't make mistakes; it's always families who are at fault. It seems that the only way this "agenda to family failure" is revealed is if a poor parent finds themselves ensnared in it. By then, it's too late. The narrative and allegations have morphed into something so preposterous that no reasonable person can believe it.

Quite honestly, I don't think I'd have ever believed something like birth alerts existed if I hadn't experienced them myself. How ridiculous! A birth alert activated on an unborn child!? My grandchild was almost taken the moment she was born.

Once my radar was tuned into these cases in 2017, I regularly heard about birth alerts and newborn babies being scooped up by social workers at the hospital.

Who the hell gave these people that kind of power? The taxpaying, voting Canadian public?

The power to assess and judge in mere minutes, making decisions for which the consequences last the rest of a child's life? I sure don't consent to this kind of imbalance.

What if something happens during labour, as is often the case? Perhaps a C-section is required and the mom isn't even conscious while a birth alert has been activated! She wakes up to find that her baby was kidnapped while she slept. How is she supposed to sift through the hazy confusion of surgery and social workers' vague reasons why her newborn was taken? How can she possibly mount a proper defence in court? Has she even had time to talk to a lawyer?

The MCFD will criminalize her poverty, dig up all the things she did wrong since third grade, and placate her instinct to be one with her baby by telling her the baby is "better off" with a good family—in other words, a family with a "mommy and daddy," never mind the fact that they're foster strangers paid by the government.

How does this mom prove her love for her baby in court?

On paper?

It's impossible, and it's not a fair fight.

Social workers seem quite comfortable slapping labels on people,[15] yet they are dismissive of a child "who doesn't have a chance." In other words, CPS knows this kid is in danger with rotten parents, but there's nothing they can (or will) do to protect the child. Social workers know they will have a hard time building a case against these parents because they learned how to "play the system." They know to ensure their home is staged properly when a social worker comes to visit, with beer bottles cleaned up and a fridge full of food. They learn this from their parents.

That child is precisely the child that the MCFD and CPS should be protecting and monitoring on a regular basis, but they're so busy with the industrious job of filling "warehouse wastelands" with as many children as possible, they don't have the time for the child who truly needs protection. *That child* is precisely who I want to invest my tax dollars in to help lift them out of their situation. I don't want my money going to some faceless "crown corporation with taxpayer-funded shareholders" holding the keys to the vault.

Aren't social workers supposed to use special skills when trying to assess if children truly need protection? Aren't they supposed to be objective when viewing a home, looking for clues as to whether the home is "staged" or not?

Any good social worker, one who truly wanted to help the family as a whole, was eclipsed long ago. Suzanne had one such social worker, Jude McLellan, who could see that Teddy and Derek were cared for and loved by her. After the boys were taken from Suzanne, Jude was replaced by another worker who knew nothing of Suzanne's history of caring for both boys since birth and her desire to legally adopt them.

Two books, *The Worst Interests of the Child* by Keith Harmon Snow and *Legally Kidnapped Children* by W. Howe, discuss good social workers quitting because the job wasn't what they had

---

[15]   *The label that the MCFD seemed to slap on my daughter was that of "poor white trash." She might be poor, and she is white, but she is certainly not trash. She was brought up in love, and my grandchild will be, too.*

signed up for. And another book, *Legally Kidnapped* by former social worker Carlos Morales, is a must-read for anyone dealing with CPS. It gives the reader an inside look at CPS when Morales worked there.

In another book, Deborah K. Frontiera is a grandmother like me. She dealt with Texas CPS with regard to her grandson and wrote a book about it called *Fighting CPS*. In the book, she describes meeting one of many social workers. Frontiera raised three children who are now grown and is a grandmother and a teacher with twenty-plus years of experience, yet this social worker asked Frontiera if she would like any "parenting" tips. Frontiera asked if she had children of her own and her response was "No."

I am calling BS on this whole ridiculous thing. Who do these people think they are? Offering to give parenting tips when she's not even a parent herself!?

Frontiera continues to be very diplomatic in her book, citing instances where CPS was needed, as she definitely would've seen a thing or two as a teacher for so many years.

I'm not anywhere nearly as diplomatic. I try to be, but I have very little patience for stupidity and a lack of common sense. I have even less patience for people who seem to get off on having "the power of God" to take children by the questionable tactics I've witnessed.

I've already questioned the ethics of having a government ministry, which has the power to apprehend children, also be in charge of who gets to adopt these children. CPS machines, like the MCFD, operate on one main principle: he who controls the children controls the money. *Control* in the MCFD vernacular means *custody*.

Referring back to the book *Legally Kidnapped Children*, Howe shares an inside look into CPS by a social worker with knowledge of his case. Though it appears that Howe is self-published, I looked past the presentation of his book and read the content. It is heartbreaking. This social worker seemed powerless to help:

As of today, I resigned. I cannot be a part of this madness anymore. You see, each year, between March 1 and November 1, if a family receives some sort of "low-income funding,"[16] it is mandatory that we remove 500 children from non-abusive homes. It is easy to adopt those kinds of children versus children with problems. Nine out of ten children we remove are from good families. No one wants to adopt children with issues. Sure, we occasionally rescue genuinely abused children to keep a positive image to the public.[17] God knows what would happen if they really knew the truth. We hire young college female graduates with no ties to children. It makes it easy for them to take children because these young women have no maternal instincts yet. We train them to be your friends, so you are more relaxed around them.

Though this author and excerpt are from the United States, every "whistle-blowing" word this social worker admitted makes me say, yet again, I'm calling BS on this madness!

This is exactly how the MCFD acted toward my daughter. And if I hadn't shown up when I did, they would have continued to treat my daughter in this two-faced way until they got what they wanted: the almighty signature and Bianca. Our baby.

Social workers do not have the power of God. They do not get to choose who gets to be parents and who doesn't. But that's exactly what they're doing. Bianca is exactly where she's supposed to be: with her loving mother. And Derek and Teddy? Suzanne doesn't know where they are to this day. The MCFD had no right

---

[16] *The quotations are mine, and here's why. Ministries like the MCFD are able to predetermine the poorest of the poor. They have access to provincial records and, in my opinion, breach people's privacy by forming opinions and prepping a child protection case long before the parents have seen the inside of a courtroom. The MCFD knows that marginalized families won't be able to afford lawyers and probably have very little education. I doubt many of them would've gone as far as I did, working with Rogerson Law Group, asking questions about the presentation of evidence and what is reasonable with regard to the sharing of personal information, birth alerts, and other bodily samples that the MCFD is able to extract from mothers.*

[17] *This was one of my husband's pet peeves, and I will address it later.*

to take those boys, certainly not if their policies are supposed to be acting "in the best interests of the child." It makes my blood boil that they just became statistics, two more boys added to the countless number of children bouncing around the foster care system. They had a chance at a good and happy life, and now it's gone. The MCFD took it from them.

Writing our story and talking about Suzanne's loss of Derek and Teddy has been cathartic for me—and Suzanne, too. She has buried so much pain and regret, and she would've never had the wherewithal to do this alone. When her boys were taken away from her, she needed a team like my daughter had to help get her child back. Suzanne didn't have a team then, but she does now.

Every poor parent caught in this system needs one. There needs to be more balance and fairness, not just the rigged, one-sided system it is today. Parents do not bring children into this world only to have bar codes slapped onto their foreheads. My daughter and I would've never stopped looking for our baby girl if the MCFD had been able to successfully keep her in the system. Teddy and Derek would be doing well today with Suzanne's love and care and a big brother to look up to. Instead, the MCFD got involved and they simply vanished.

7

MICHELLE

Just after Bianca's second birthday, I was on a Facebook support group I had found during our time in fancy prison. These cases were now on my radar, and I would try to read about someone's story whenever I had free time. CPS seems to play a numbers game. Of the very few families who do win and get their kids back, there is still a fraction of that fraction who are in a (financial) position to sue. The vast majority rarely get any form of justice or compensation for what social workers put them through, whether they get their children back or not.

I was hoping to be that fraction of the fraction, but it's easier said than done. Our lives were moving on, and it wasn't like I was sitting around waiting for our lawyer to call. By the time I was ready to write this book, Dan had died and I had retained Rogerson Law Group. I made it very clear that I wanted to sue the MCFD. But the only thing that moves fast in this stupid system is how quickly they apprehend children.

Everything else is at a snail's pace, from court procedures to Freedom of Information applications to reticent lawyers who aren't usually interested in going up against government. It's very easy for the statute of limitations to run out. And as Rogerson Law Group stated in their report in Chapter 4, I would "not be entitled to the same disclosure rights afforded to my daughter" with regard to any lawsuit. My daughter didn't have the time or money to pursue legal action. By then, Bianca was a full-fledged toddler. It's my daughter's turn to be the busy, single mom raising a child. I, on the other hand, had the time and money to seek some kind of justice and compensation.

On this Facebook support group, I was reading about a particular case. It struck a chord with me as to the similarities with my daughter's case. I asked this mom, Michelle, a couple of questions. She answered back and then asked me some questions. I answered back with some advice. Thus began a pen pal relationship that has lasted to this day. Michelle is still dealing with the MCFD. For this reason, her and her children's names have been changed, and I'll keep the details vague without losing the truth of her ordeal. Michelle has two children: her daughter, Haley, and her son, Michael, who is a couple of years younger than his sister. Both have the same father.

There were two main differences between Michelle's case and my daughter's. Firstly, Michelle did not have a good relationship with her parents. Rather than "work with" families in what's best for the care of the children, the MCFD will exploit this familial discord. Secondly, her children were school-aged and old enough to voice their own opinions.

It didn't take long for me to realize that Michelle was an intelligent, articulate person who loved her children very much. And just because she didn't get along with her parents didn't mean that she had no support. She did. She had friends and advocates who helped her with her fight against the MCFD, and now she had me as an ally. I knew the avalanche of paperwork that social workers would slide in front of her, expecting her signature. Michelle signed nothing. She had a lawyer and, just like us, dug in for a fight.

Remember, I'd only been dealing with this system for a few years. Suzanne had a couple of decades' worth of experience, so I always ran my texts of advice by her before sending them to Michelle. You might wonder why Suzanne didn't just communicate directly with Michelle. She couldn't. Suzanne will always grieve the loss of Teddy and Derek. It doesn't help her grief by continuing to be involved in these cases. Grieving the loss of children who are still alive is as unnatural as it is for parents to have to bury their child. Everyone grieves in their own way.

Suzanne, however, was totally comfortable with having me as a buffer during this type of communication. With all her heart, Suzanne wanted to give advice to help Michelle, a complete stranger, but she needed to protect her boundaries as well.

Haley and Michael were apprehended by the MCFD and placed with their grandparents in the spring of 2019, with still a couple more months of school to go. Michelle was extremely stressed and frustrated by this. She didn't get along with them, her mother in particular, and her protests were ignored by everyone involved when her children were made to sleep on couches. By June, Michelle and her lawyer had tried giving the MCFD plenty of opportunities to return Haley and Michael to their mother. But the MCFD would have none of it.

Dad was in the picture, but he had never been the primary caregiver. By apprehending Haley and Michael, the MCFD controlled who got (temporary) custody and who got to visit them. Michelle had never prevented her children from spending time with their father. The MCFD's invasion into parental visits, both hers and the father's, wasn't necessary and seemed to only inflame Michelle's distress and cause further discord.

Time and time again, I read about these cases and opportunities that the MCFD has to genuinely "work with" families, and all they seem to do is cause more harm, particularly to the children. I really don't understand how a child screaming for his or her mother can fall on deaf ears, but it does.

I call BS on this system. It is inhuman.

Again, the reasons were vague as to why Michelle's children were apprehended. The MCFD insinuated that Michelle *might* use recreational drugs and that Michelle *might* have a breakdown as a single mom. It's ridiculous how these "crystal ball" predictions are made against parents, but they are. And they work.

Parent after parent after parent is hauled into court to face CPS based only on social workers' presumptive predictions.

I communicated regularly with Michelle during the summer of 2019. Her kids were out of school, and her parents worked full-time. Their "care" during the day caused Michelle a considerable amount of anxiety. Though the MCFD did nothing to check on the kids' stability, as they seemed to be still sleeping on couches, they cared even less about Michelle's concerns for her children. She had lots of questions for me.

We texted back and forth. Michelle would describe her concerns. I would copy and paste my response first to Suzanne. Suzanne and I had a side discussion on what Michelle's questions were, and I would tweak my response accordingly before sending it back to Michelle. We were discussing someone's children, so the importance of the advice we were giving Michelle was never lost on us.

This type of three-way communication is time-consuming. I work as a fundraising coordinator for not-for-profits, and the campaign I was working on at that time was for homeless youth (www.osys.ca). Though I was supposed to be doing my job, giving the right advice to Michelle was just as important. In fact, I'd like to think it was more important from a prevention point of view.

The statistics linking homeless youth to the foster care system are undeniable. Some of these statistics are outlined in the book *The Youth in Care Chronicles*,[18] which came out in the last part of 2020. Over half of the youth who grew up in foster care end up living on the streets by age sixteen.

Their health and education suffer, too. They are over 35 percent more likely to be assigned a learning disability than students from non-foster homes, and this may very well have contributed to this next stat. Only 47 percent of youth in foster care completed high school, compared to the 84 percent graduation rate of students in the general population.

---

[18] *Penny Frazier was one of the main collaborators, and other authors helped the kids articulate their stories in this book.*

This vicious cycle spirals downward, from foster care to home-lessness, addiction, jail, and early death. Foster kids are seven times more likely to take their own lives. I will defer to the kids who survived, telling their own stories in this book.

I digress again and return to Michelle's children, who were still continuing to live in a temporary setup in their grandparents' home. It was reasonable for Michelle to think that the MCFD would eventually find a reason to move them to foster care.

By willingly giving a few hours of my time at the expense of doing my job, I think I was getting more to the root of the problem. By collaborating with Suzanne and giving Michelle our best advice possible, I helped a mom oppose the MCFD, gaining the upper hand with regard to Haley and Michael's future. After a year and a half of going back and forth, texting with Michelle during peak stressful times and low routine times, a judge finally ended it.

Just like us, Michelle had finally gotten one with common sense. The judge ruled, on a glorious day in court in the autumn of 2020, that Michelle's children would be returned to her custody. She texted me later that day.

I was ecstatic to hear the news, and so was Suzanne.

Their systematic way of apprehending children hadn't worked on Michelle. Just like my daughter, she had had a support team that helped her persevere. It took her eighteen months—twice as long as we had to endure the MCFD—but Michelle got Haley and Michael back.

There is one major issue I'd like to emphasize, and it is that Michelle's children were school-aged. It just adds a tremendous amount of confusion and is pure manipulation that a social worker can blindside a child by showing up at their school to "interrogate" them. Haley and Michael were pulled out of class regularly due to the MCFD's continued interference. Imagine how that child feels, being singled out in front of their class. They are interviewed without the teacher or any other adult present. The MCFD can ask pointed questions and "cherry-pick" what a child says to suit their specific narrative.

Children don't react to authority the same way adults do. If asked pointed, leading questions, their answers can easily be misinterpreted. Social workers will repeatedly ask the child the same thing, over and over, by simply wording it differently. Eventually, a child believes they keep getting asked the same question because they're not giving the "correct" answer. Thereby, a social worker can *lead* a child's answers into fitting the narrative they want, and no one is the wiser. There is no recording and no one there to advocate for the child.

Parents usually don't find out their child was questioned by social workers until later that day, after school, if they find out at all. Most, understandably, are furious.

Parents are already stressed and humiliated at having the MCFD involved in their lives, so just in case every classmate doesn't already know it, the MCFD's final nail in the coffin is this overarching power they have to seriously disrupt a child's day at school. Often, the information they gain by these questionable methods is enough to seriously disrupt the rest of the child's life.

Fortunately, for Michelle and her children that turned out to not be the case. For now. She still lives in fear of her children not returning home from school.

8

THE TIME-TRAVELLING EAGLE

Expecting your children to come home each day after school is a given as parents, yet for many families whose children were ordered by the government of Canada to attend residential schools, this homecoming never happened.

In a book about child protection, I would be remiss if I didn't at least touch on the government policies impacting the First Nations of this land. Though I am loath to point this out, because I believe *all* children are born equal with inherent rights in the eyes of God, it is the system that differentiates Indigenous children. It does so on the endless forms with all the "ticky boxes" and categories they assign to families.

The disproportionately high number of Indigenous children in the Canadian CPS system is undeniable. Of the five children I've discussed so far—Bianca, Derek, Teddy, Haley, and Michael—four of them had at least one parent of Indigenous origins. Similar to my small baseline, 80 percent is reflective of the proportion that Indigenous children make up in government care. Yet, the fraction that Indigenous children represent compared to the overall population of minors in Canada is about 10 percent.

I cannot even begin to provide "solutions" regarding each and every case for each and every child. It isn't fair to expect that of me. I'm just one grammy who is writing a book about our ordeal. I will draw a comparison, though, by circling back to the commonality of schooling. Let's start with the fact that more than 150,000 Indigenous children were separated from their families and put into residential schools.

The first of these schools opened in Canada in 1831, and the last one closed as recently as 1997. That's a span of 166 years and, in my fifty-seven years on this earth, I've only heard of one lady who had a good experience when she went to residential school. Most survivors recount the abuses they suffered, physical, emotional, and sexual. The majority of these schools made a clear distinction between the chores expected from boys and girls. Boys were sent outdoors to do the work of ranch hands and farmers, while girls cooked and cleaned inside. They had neither the energy nor the incentive to do the work of an adult, as they were given porridge morning, noon, and night. It often had maggots in it—sometimes even mouse droppings! As unbelievably disgusting as that is, the children were told to eat it or starve. Some did.

The priests and nuns who ran these schools were sustained by robust meals. Imagine this contrast. The children's mouths would water when seeing and smelling this delicious food, and then their eyes would water, too, at the aching injustice of it. Adults were served healthy food, while growing children had to eat shit.

I was once told, in a rather matter-of-fact way, that it was usually an older boy who would be assigned a special task. Since the boys were sent outdoors, one would be assigned the task of digging graves. Many of the children sent to residential schools never came home. They died there. I cannot imagine what it would've been like for a young man, assigned this morbid task, to be sitting beside a classmate one day and having to bury him the next day.

And it seems to be common knowledge, passed on by Indigenous elders, that it was not unheard of for a child to be buried alive! That poor soul was instructed to keep digging the grave and fill it in, even though the other poor soul, a child, wasn't dead. They were just extremely ill. It's unclear to me, when I try to process this heinous act, whether or not the priests and nuns knew that the child needed a doctor, not a gravedigger.

I suspect this confusion would've been the children's as well.

It certainly doesn't sound like there was very much learning going on. "Surviving" residential school is how it is aptly viewed, because all these schools managed to do was inflict mystifying new rules on the children in a language they couldn't understand. They were exposed to new diseases and were banned from practising their cultural and religious teachings, depriving them of their personal identity and freedoms. Sometimes brothers and sisters couldn't even talk to each other, especially if their sleeping quarters were kept separated by gender. The children were forbidden to speak—whether in their native tongue or any other—while in class.

There are many advocacy groups in Canada that are striving to right the wrongs committed to these children, who are now adults. If they did survive the horrors of residential schools, many have died since then. I suspect some of those who remain have never spoken about what happened to them as children, and they never will. Their feelings of shame, though not even remotely their fault, are something they'd rather just carry to their graves.

It is absolutely impossible to measure the residual damage this kind of trauma would have on a child, their future children, their communities, and their capacity to contribute. It's impossible to get to the root of a problem when the untreated trauma is not even acknowledged. The confusion, then and now, perpetuates. I do think it would be irresponsible to put these atrocities "in the past," as they continue, in a different form, in the current child welfare industry and its high proportion of Indigenous children.

I let my imagination wander at times, while reading or watching a movie. I wonder what Canada must've been like in the early 1800s. If I were a time-travelling eagle, I would see villages, perhaps like what John Dunbar saw in *Dances with Wolves*. Look up and see this eagle soaring along the Bow River on a spring day in 1826.

The songbirds and the rising sun bid "good morning" to the people as winter's weariness is beat off teepees and furs. The village's very survival depended on each and every person staying together, closely huddled and out of the wind, with a constant watch on the wood supply to keep the fires going.

With the dawn of spring, families wake and look up, wondering if the eagle can see if storm clouds are climbing up the Rocky Mountains, heading east toward their village. Grandpa slowly walks on creaky knees, hand in hand with his grandchild, to fetch some fresh water. As the grandparent walks, he talks and the child listens. They see green buds starting to burst forth in the trees and the whiteness of clouds in a blue sky.

Perhaps Grandpa has an explanation for the different shades of blue in the sky? We skip stones by the river and realize we must hurry to get the water back to our waiting mother. Mother scolds me for taking so long, with everyone waiting for some breakfast.

The child's head hangs low with this scolding. Grandpa has an impish smile, knowing the tardiness is mostly his fault but knowing elders do not get scolded like children.

I cannot think of a more beautiful way for children to learn: with love and gentle words from the elder and disciplinary direction from the parent. Seeing their fathers hunt and fish and their mothers prepare meals and stores for the winter come autumn is the magical rhythm of nature and a tactile environment where children learn and have an opportunity to absorb every detail around them. When Grandpa and Grandma die, the children follow another elder and listen to the knowledge being passed on to them.

Tell me what the eagle does not see?

Books.

In fact, it's the very need that John Dunbar has to keep a journal that is the climax of the story in *Dances with Wolves*. The very fact that I can share our ordeal in the form of this book is just a by-product of the upbringing I had and my access to education. I wasn't sent away to school and could come home each afternoon on the bus. My mother cooked and cleaned and called us in for dinner at six o'clock. She learned this from her mother, growing up in Italy.

Just like the Italian culture factored heavily in my upbringing, so too does the culture of Indigenous peoples factor into theirs. They have a strong connection to their ancestors and a different understanding of the spirit world. It has long been known that Indigenous people connect with one another through songs, ceremonies, dance, and storytelling and, quite simply, it is not my place to tell their story. It is my sincere hope that saying very little on this matter says it all.

9

DELONNA SULLIVAN

A few years ago, I attended a child protection forum. It was the first time I'd heard about Delonna Sullivan.

Delonna's mother, Jamie, was a single mom with no fortune and a great capacity for love. She remains united in grief with her mother, Marilyn, and their presentation at this child protection forum displayed lots of photos of a beautiful baby with hazel eyes. Delonna's grandmother Marilyn did most of the talking, and Jamie sat in front of the photographs of her baby girl. I won't attempt to try to describe what is only Jamie's grief to bear.

I hung on every word Marilyn spoke.

Sometime in late March or early April of 2011, Jamie had had a fight with her roommate's teenage daughter. It was a common occurrence with this girl. Jamie had to share the house she rented with another single mom so she could make ends meet. Delonna's father was long gone. This other single mom had three children, including the teenager. After her fight with Jamie, the teenager left the house.

A few weeks later, Alberta social workers out of Leduc County arrived at Jamie's home. To Jamie's surprise, her roommate didn't put up much of a fight when social workers apprehended her kids. Then they saw Delonna. They did not even know about this four-month-old baby, so it was logical to assume that the call placed to them was not a protection concern about Delonna.

She was carelessly and recklessly scooped up with the rest of the children. Unlike her roommate, Jamie's mama bear instinct kicked in and she put up a fight. *On what grounds? Where's the court order?* There couldn't possibly be one, certainly nothing with Delonna Sullivan's name on it. They didn't even know of her existence.

Alberta social services didn't even have a baby car seat for nineteen-pound Delonna. Jamie was distraught that social workers were about to drive off with her baby, even without a safe car seat. They threatened Jamie with jail time, even though there was a police officer with them who was supposed to be *protecting* Delonna Sullivan!

The social workers intimated, "We can do this the hard way or the easy way." Realizing that "the hard way" meant trying to be reunited with her baby from jail, Jamie conceded and gave them Delonna's car seat. She was sure this was all a mistake, and her baby would be returned in no time.

Little did she know...

What happened in the next week after Delonna was taken is the most heinous act inflicted on an innocent child and her family and is another reason why I'm calling BS on this whole vile industry.

Delonna Sullivan was taken on April 5, 2011, which was a Tuesday. Jamie and Marilyn did not get their first visit until Friday. They immediately noticed that Delonna was sick. She was lethargic and not her usual happy baby self. They begged the foster "thing"[19] to take her to emergency. She was dismissive of Jamie's maternal concern for her baby's health. The foster thing said she'd wait until Monday to see if Delonna was better and then make an appointment.

---

[19] *Their version of our winky-face Kathy. "Thing" is what they call the stranger who was supposed to be taking care of their baby. They refuse to call her "foster mother."*

This wasn't good enough for Jamie. She kept following up with social services, who were supposed to meet with her and Marilyn on Friday after their visit with Delonna. The social worker didn't show. Jamie was desperate for someone to take her seriously and to have her baby seen by a doctor immediately. The stress was unbearable. Friday, April 8, 2011, will be forever etched in Jamie's memory. It was the last time she saw her baby alive. As Delonna was carried away by the foster thing, she pleadingly looked back at her mother. Jamie's broken heart went with her.

In my experience, these ministries just don't give a shit how parents feel. Families are all slapped with a "guilty" label without any due process before even seeing the inside of a courtroom. Court for Jamie was set for Tuesday, April 12. Delonna Sullivan never made it to that day.

The foster thing testified later that she had put Delonna down for a nap between 9 and 10 a.m. on April 11. She still hadn't made a doctor's appointment to have Delonna looked at. She heard noises coming from behind the closed door of the room, where Delonna was in a crib. The foster thing's recollections were vague, but she thought maybe it was around noon. She did not check on Delonna until 3:30 that afternoon. The baby was dead.

Aren't foster parents supposed to keep more accurate records and journals about the children in their care? Why can't this foster parent remember exactly when Delonna was put down for her nap? Why didn't she check on the baby when she heard sounds? Doesn't she, as a foster parent, have first aid and CPR training? What happened the next day in court? Was the case of Delonna Sullivan called before the judge? Did the judge know that this perfectly healthy baby had died the day before? Did the judge ever find out that Delonna, who weighed nineteen pounds when she was taken from her mother, weighed only thirteen pounds a week later when an autopsy was done on her little body? Did the judge or any ensuing fatality inquiry ever question why Delonna had an excessive dosage of medication that should never have been given to a child so young?

And the biggest question of all: Why was Delonna Sullivan taken from her mother in the first place?

To this day, no one has ever been held accountable for Delonna Sullivan's death. Within a week of social workers walking into Jamie's home, with their clipboards and air of intimidation, a four-month-old baby was dead. A family was destroyed.

Rather than have to embark on the routine "hoop jumping" that CPS makes all parents go through, Jamie and Marilyn had to plan a funeral for their baby girl. They had to let Delonna go, lay her in a tiny pink coffin, and lower her into the ground.

At this child protection forum I attended, when Marilyn recounted their experience, I couldn't bear to listen. I knew the trajectory of where this was going. The foster "parent" was never charged. Social services circled the wagons, protecting their own.

I left the room in tears. I went to the bathroom and just sat in a stall with the door closed. I didn't need to use the toilet, but I did need to be alone. The old Tina would've had a hard time believing what happened to Delonna Sullivan. The new Tina didn't.

When I left the bathroom to rejoin the forum, I could hardly bear to look into Jamie's eyes. But she met my gaze, somehow understanding my departure, and this mother who suffered the worst grief a parent can bear gave *me* a hug. I remembered the words of my longtime friend in Banff. She said that whoever initiates the hug has to let go first.

I let Jamie hug me as long as she wanted.

When she did let go, she spoke about Delonna. I told her it was such a pretty name, and she explained to me where it came from. I don't recall exactly *what* she said, but I remember well *how* she said it. She was so calm. There was no anger in her voice, only love. Like I said, I won't attempt to describe a pain that is only Jamie's, but I do think that speaking about Delonna is how she and her mother honour the memory of their precious little girl. They remain united in grief and continue to talk about

Delonna at child protection events like these, raising awareness and seeking answers to what was done to their baby girl.

While my regrets pale in comparison to theirs, I do have a few and, fortunately, they don't keep me up at night.

Enough

10

HINDSIGHT IS 20/20

The number one regret is that I should have had a lawyer. I suspect that most of you who've read my book so far have already figured that out. You must think I'm a real dummy for not doing my homework and retaining a lawyer ASAP. But here's the thing. That first week when I started communicating with the MCFD and Suzanne was there by my daughter's side, I was given a false sense of security. Winky-face Kathy made it seem like "we're all on the same page," probably to keep me at bay. They wanted to ensure that I remained in Alberta so the MCFD could be free to conduct their systematic routine of setting my daughter up to fail.

It was Suzanne who summoned me, knowing exactly what the MCFD was up to. Once upon a time, I had not even heard of the MCFD, what the acronym stood for, and the confusion that is CPS.

When Suzanne summoned me, I remembered asking her if I should pack something to wear to court.

Definitely!

Court is where we should've been able to defend ourselves. I, in particular, had had no complaint lodged against me. Why was I to be interrogated and constantly hauled into court? Social workers treated me like I was "guilty" and like I had no legal right to my grandchild. I kept copies of emails from winky-face Kathy, which she usually sent at closing time on Fridays. It would be notice of the next court date coming up, within days, and she would state in each of her emails, "You do not have to attend court if you sign the written consents and get them back to me."

Yeah, right. I'm sure the MCFD would've loved that: to have us not show up for court so they could narrate *their* version of *our* story to the judge and have us continuously, mindlessly sign whatever they put in front of us.

So, that very first week with winky-face Kathy, when she had stalled and rescheduled our first meeting several times, I should have cut through the BS and gone to see a lawyer ASAP. I should have brought said lawyer with me and just paid him or her out of my pocket. It would've saved me thousands of dollars down the road because maybe—*just maybe*—the MCFD would've backed off and given me and my daughter some breathing space and freedom to do what I knew needed to be done.

My daughter needed a place to call her own. She didn't need to be in a chaotic household with four other children running around, with the mother at a convenient vantage point to spy on my daughter (it seems) on behalf of the MCFD.

And I say *maybe* because the presence of a lawyer may not have mattered. The MCFD has reigned terror on families for so long and with such impunity that having a lawyer with me may not have made a difference. For the social workers, the knowledge that they were being recorded didn't stop them from apprehending Bianca. I still have that recording and, as far as I'm concerned, it is proof of the crime of kidnapping. Social workers had no right to take my granddaughter from me! At the very least, Bianca should've been given to me while the MCFD sorted out their issues with my daughter.[20]

---

[20] *If I haven't already made it clear, these issues and reasons for taking the baby and keeping her in the system would constantly change, depending on what stage in the "game" plan we were in.*

This leads to my second regret: I should have acted and dragged my and my daughter's asses down to the local RCMP[21] detachment and filed kidnapping charges on the night of Friday, March 10, 2017. My daughter was distraught and shattered, not knowing where her two-week-old baby was, so it would've been up to me to initiate this. It would've been better than what I did: lie in bed in the fetal position in absolute shock at what had just happened.

The cops probably wouldn't have done a damned thing anyway. But by not taking a kidnapping allegation seriously and doing nothing, they would have at least given me grounds for a lawsuit against law enforcement.

However, it would've been a double-edged sword. If I'd gone with my daughter to the police to file kidnapping charges, the MCFD would've clamped down on us with even less mercy, if that would've even been possible. As it was, we beat them within a year, which is a very short time compared to other cases. Many parents who endure social workers dragging out their cases unnecessarily for months, which turn into years, do not get their children back.

I'd like to know how we got here as a society, where strangers are allowed to rule supreme and make decisions about a child who doesn't belong to them. The media certainly doesn't cover it. Ministries like the MCFD hide behind the idea that "we're protected by laws to not reveal the child's identity," so it's next to impossible to gather statistics and get an idea of how big of a problem this is. This "smoke and mirrors" attitude perpetuates a fun house for the MCFD and a haunted house for the parents.

A media "circus" certainly happens when that one aberrant parent murders their own child. They're all over that, in painstaking detail, interviewing everyone from the neighbours to the third-grade teacher.

It skews public perception to have such lopsided coverage of "child needing protection" cases. It feeds the myth of "Well,

---

[21] *RCMP stands for Royal Canadian Mounted Police.*

the MCFD must have their reasons for taking these children," and the public isn't allowed to ask questions, even if it is in the spirit of objectivity. Anyone asking questions is met with "We can't discuss a case involving children," which gives them a "free pass" on their behaviour. A child's name can be easily changed, as I've done in this book, and an investigation of the actions of taxpayer-funded government staff is what is paramount.

The lack of media was one of my husband's pet peeves. Marilyn, Delonna's grandmother, agrees with him. She said as much in one of our conversations and added that parents who kill their own children get charged under the Criminal Code of Canada, as they should be. But it doesn't explain why charges were never laid in the death of her grandchild, Delonna. It doesn't explain why charges are rarely, if ever, laid when a child dies in foster care. You'd think this shocking double standard would be headline news.

It isn't.

I don't believe it's because Canadians don't care. I believe it's because they are led to believe a lie that the parents did something so heinous as to *deserve* to have a dead child. As if anyone deserves anything so cruel, the least of which is a child's life cut short.

My husband is a practical man and for him, at times, it boils down to money. He realizes that it's his tax dollars paying for this travesty and he doesn't like it one bit.

Neither should you.

Another one of my husband's pet peeves was an ethical situation that the MCFD created. When he went through our file, obtained through FOIPPA shortly after Bianca'a first birthday, my husband suspected who had made the original complaint against my daughter. He suspected it was the mother of the four children who lived upstairs in the shithole house that passed for "adequate" accommodation, according to MCFD standards.

Perhaps it was easier for social workers to overlook a mouse-infested, overcrowded house if they knew they had a built-in "spy" who could report back to them. Is that why the MCFD put these two parents in a position of "authority" over my daughter in government-sanctioned "safety plan" documents?

My husband thought this was the biggest ethical issue: to have the person or persons who made the initial call against my daughter be in a position of power over her in a legal document. After he relayed his suspicions to my daughter, she cut off all communication with them. It just wasn't worth the risk giving the "spy" even one tiny tidbit of information about her current life and how well her and Bianca were doing.

By the way, that family living upstairs fled town a few weeks after Bianca was apprehended. No doubt they were worried their kids would be next.

It is difficult to understand why the MCFD would think this potential conflict of interest would be okay. But I guess when you look at these cases and how long they've been allowed to fester and perpetuate, then you can see how the MCFD would justify that the original caller could also be their spy. Convenience over ethics.

My husband feels that setting someone up to fail like this defies any sort of logic, especially when what's at stake is the future of a child. But we dispensed with logic a long time ago when dealing with the MCFD.

It seems that the only common sense we experienced was by that wonderful judge presiding over our last court date in September 2017. We need more like him. In Chapter 8, I mentioned advocacy groups trying to right the wrongs of residential schooling. I also mentioned advocacy work like "court watching" and McKenzie Friends in Chapter 5. Before I head into my concluding chapters, I would like to touch on advocacy.

The first name that comes to mind with regard to advocacy for Indigenous children is Cindy Blackstock. She has been a force in raising awareness and funds through the First Nations Child & Family Caring Society. Blackstock spearheaded Jordan's Principle, named for Jordan River Anderson, who was born with a rare disability and lived to just the tender age of five. Jordan spent his short life in hospital and hadn't set foot in his family home in the northern Cree community of Norway House, Manitoba. At two years old, while he lay in hospital, a dispute broke out between Canadian federal and provincial governments. The issue was, who's going to pay for Jordan's medical care?

In Canada, getting medical care is free. Taxpayers contribute to the health care system, with most people requiring nothing more than annual checkups and doctors investigating further if they feel their patient's common cold is masking something more serious. Its philosophy is to treat the human first and worry about the paperwork later. Except, it seems, in the case of Jordan. The bureaucratic dispute that ensued for three of the five short years of Jordan's life was never resolved. Jordan River Anderson fell into a coma and slipped away from his family's loving arms.

Blackstock continues to work with communities, Indigenous leaders, and non-Indigenous allies, focusing mostly on children as she travels with a teddy bear companion called Spirit Bear. In addition to Jordan's Principle, some of her other initiatives are Have a Heart Day, Bear Witness Day, and Honouring Memories, Planting Dreams. More about the First Nations Child & Family Caring Society can be found at www.fncaringsociety.com.

Blackstock seems like a formidable woman, and I would very much like to meet her someday.

Another lady I'd like to meet is Helen with www.kidsfirstcanada.org. This advocacy group was involved with a case that had dragged on for years and made headlines in Vancouver, B.C. It became known as the "bus dad story." A quick Google search can enlighten readers on the details of this case and this father's persistence. He pursued what he thought was right and ended up being instrumental in a precedent decision that would help parents assert their autonomy. All of the legal fees that this father paid for came out of his own pocket.

These are just a couple of advocacy groups, but there is still much work to be done to lift families out of the marginalized situations they find themselves in. I fear that this will only have gotten worse after COVID-19.

My advice, if you find yourself desperate in a situation with CPS, is to stay away from government-funded advocacy. They may say all the right things to gain your trust, but I suspect that much of it is lip service. Their true allegiance is to the government body that funds them, so it isn't "the child's best interest" they're focused on. They're more interested in keeping the status quo and their jobs. I lost count of how many parents complained that going to the provincial child advocate was useless. Canadian bureaucratic inertia paralyzes any real kind of action. They seemed enslaved to "the system" as they routinely put paperwork before people. It's best to turn to advocates like the First Nations Child & Family Caring Society and Children First Canada, which are run by passionate people who are working out of the kindness of their hearts.

I did start a charity after our ordeal, and anything I dedicate to it is done in my free time. Like everyone else in the pandemic, the past year has been challenging for my "day job" of fundraising for non-profits. I mention my charity only to make a point. Its mission has morphed and changed in my thoughts over the years, but its essence remains a legal advocacy at its core. So much of what the MCFD does can be cut short if parents have a good lawyer from the very start. Chances are, these parents have been exploited because of their poverty, and it is truly tragic that the people who are in most need of justice are the ones who are least able to afford it.

My charitable notion wouldn't be to ensure that each and every parent gets their children back—some children truly do need protection—but to ensure that parents can prepare for a fair fight in court. I will refer back to Chapter 4, where I highlighted that parents are treated like guilty criminals and denied the basic legal principle of innocent until proven guilty. I would love nothing more than for my charitable work to help "level the playing field" to ensure that parents have fair and proper legal help. One by one is how each case is supposed to be approached, not the wholesale "one-size-fits-all" attitude that CPS seems okay with now. Each family needs to be able to access the resources to make it a fair fight in court. I think then, the tides would begin to turn.

11

2021

Poor families have had enough. My husband and I are not poor, but we certainly had had enough of the MCFD by the time Bianca was seven months old in September 2017. We had resources to help my daughter, despite CPS trying to disrupt our family dynamic by pitting me against my own child. Divide and conquer. The stress was overwhelming and would not have been sustainable. My daughter would've needed me more than ever if her child had been lost. The MCFD would've surely cost me my marriage, not that they cared. My husband's confusion, though more delayed than ours, was no less potent. After that wonderful judge asked us to try to sort it out on that final court day, my husband asked winky-face Kathy and the MCFD lawyer, point blank, "How is causing the mother emotional and monetary stress in the best interest of the child?"

My husband's frustration and questioning were met with silence. The lawyer ignored him. As for winky-face Kathy, about an hour after my husband posed this question, she begrudgingly admitted to the judge that the MCFD saw no problems with my daughter keeping her child. Geez, it only took seven months for the MCFD to say this in court, and it did not come freely. She was *forced* to admit this when she realized that we had gotten the kind of judge we needed and His Honour wasn't putting up with anymore of the MCFD's stall tactics. (Carrying Bianca into court with us that day—so that the judge could see we weren't hiding anything—no doubt helped.)

We've been vigilant ever since 2017, just trying to undo the stress and damage that the MCFD temporarily caused. We learned a couple more shocking things in the course of trying to restore some order to our lives. First, it took us almost a year to apply for Bianca's birth certificate. When my daughter called British Columbia registries—sometime in January 2018—to get the form for her to officially proclaim her daughter's name to the world, she was told that someone had tried to register Bianca's birth! My daughter was stunned. *Who tried to do this?* They didn't know or, perhaps, weren't willing to divulge that information. *When?* Thursday, March 16, 2017. That would've been within a week of Bianca's apprehension.

To this day, we have no idea who tried to register Bianca's birth. We can only suspect that it was the MCFD. It's a valid guess, based on the timing and the circumstances. Changing Bianca's name right after she'd been apprehended would've made it impossible for me and my daughter to track where they had moved her. I think the social workers figured out early on that wherever they moved our baby, we would follow. They were right about that one thing. We would just live out of a hotel in whatever town they moved Bianca to so we could keep up visits.

For anyone dealing with CPS, this is, by far, the most important thing parents have a right to assert. If you keep showing up for visits, if you keep "trying" to work with CPS to mitigate their "concerns" (whether or not they're even true), and if you keep your cool and have the wherewithal to lawyer up and the dedication to do whatever it takes to get your child back, CPS can't "pigeon hole" you into their usual one-size-fits-all category and you have a better chance of reuniting your family. It's best if you can do this early, without signing anything.

I'm going to say that again because it's very important.

Do not sign *anything* without a lawyer explaining exactly what it is and until you've had time to read, reread, and really consider the implications of the document they slide in front of you. In British Columbia, the MCFD have to wait one year before they can apply to the courts for a continuing custody order (CCO) that doesn't have the parents' signatures on it. That's why they overwhelm parents with stress and paperwork right from the start. It is not unheard of for social workers to imply that "reunification with their child will happen once they sign the enclosed form." Winky-face Kathy sent us several emails stating variations of "generous promises." If I hadn't been there for my daughter and she had been tricked into signing a CCO, it would've been very difficult to undo.

I could go on and on here with other elaborations of what to do and not do, but every case is so very different and I'm not a lawyer. It's best to get one ASAP. I will say, though—and I truly believe—that love conquers all. Fight like hell, like your life depends on it. Because it does. At the very least, your children are counting on you to not give up.

And the best way to get—and keep—CPS out of your life is to live a life beyond reproach. I thank God every day that I didn't have some youthful indiscretion that would've cost me my grandchild. Social workers were actively looking for some dirt on me. Thankfully, I'd filled my life with books, work, and making my family a priority.

In the summer of 2018, our tenacity paid off as we found out a second shocker. It seemed that the MCFD had never informed the federal government (from which it gets its funding) that Bianca had been put into provincial custody. Within days of her baby being taken from us—around the middle of March 2017—my daughter received a letter regarding her monthly child benefit stipend. Millions of Canadian families receive this cheque around the third week of each month. The letter my daughter received stated that the monthly funding attached to Bianca's care would be redirected to provincial coffers.

In that moment, my daughter hardly cared about the money. She just wanted her baby back.

Our file closed in January of 2018, ten months after Bianca had been apprehended. My daughter had been living in her home province of Alberta for nine of those ten months. Six months with me—from April to October 2017—and three months on her own (finally) with her baby. But my daughter continued to receive bills from the B.C. government. It seemed she *owed* them money! Never mind the fact that while my daughter served her time in fancy prison, she never received those cheques. Someone with authority was intentionally withholding that money. Within a few weeks of the final court date in September 2017, my daughter received a huge cheque that included all the retroactive monthly amounts she hadn't received. When she saw the amount, her jaw hit the floor. She could pay off what rent was owed and still have enough for a damage deposit, plus first month's rent, on a place for her and Bianca.

When she showed me the cheque, I knew we had officially won. I'm sure someone at the MCFD was loath to release those funds to my daughter. They'd been banking on keeping Bianca "in the system" for God knows how long.

So, my daughter received this cheque and our file was closed. Why does she keep getting bills from British Columbia to repay them their money? It's because, according to Canada Revenue Agency (CRA), the federal government had no record of Bianca ever being in provincial care. Usually, the minute the MCFD takes a child, they do what's needed to ensure that the funding follows. That is consistent with the letter that followed Bianca's apprehension, telling my daughter that she wouldn't be eligible for the funding to care for her child. But the social workers must've seen something in us that caused them to wait. The MCFD never informed CRA of Bianca being in their custody. My daughter eventually received this confirmation in writing in a letter stating, according to their (CRA) records, my daughter "had always retained custody of her baby"!?

CONCLUSION

It just makes me shake my head at what a fucking joke this all is to them. These are innocent children caught in the bureaucratic BS known as the MCFD.

It's just been so overwhelming and stressful, in 2017 and since then, trying to process all my thoughts and feelings. I almost couldn't write this book. How could I form some sort of logical cohesion out of this madness? A book like this would demand no less. The level of stress parents experience is absolutely paralyzing. It is difficult to articulate.

But I had to try.

My catalyst arrived in an unexpected way. Though I realize it is unorthodox to mention my publisher in the story line, it is what it is. During the COVID-19 lockdowns in 2020, I found myself at home with time on my hands, like everyone else. I participated in one of Rob Kosberg's author challenges. Long story short, I won one of his publishing prizes. I just needed to write the book. Without this catalyst, I don't know if I would have ever completed it. The day after I won this prize, Suzanne said, "Tina, this isn't a coincidence. You were meant to tell your story." I know she would've never been able to tell her story about her sons, Teddy and Derek, without this book.

Our tax dollars are paying for the BS that is child welfare. So, at the very least, we have the right to start asking valid questions, like why there seems to be no money whatsoever invested in preventing families from being separated. I thought that's what social services is supposed to be: to help families who need help. Instead, families who turn to the MCFD for help end up losing their kids. Sometimes it's for the most ridiculous reasons, if those reasons are even revealed. And if they are, just wait. They will change come Friday at four o'clock.

The wholesale operation that the child welfare industry is running now, of taking children on such a massive scale, makes it damn near impossible to even find a child who truly is in danger—never mind that child actually getting protection.

Don't human rights apply to children as well?

Another thing I wasn't able to fit in our story line is the issue of addressing trauma. I merely touched on the history of residential schooling and the effect it has had on generations of Indigenous families. It is shattering for both parent and child when they are separated. This trauma, if left untreated, can rear its ugly head in other ways down the road. I think Western medicine needs to do far more in the acknowledgement and treatment of trauma. I'm not a doctor, but that's just my personal opinion—an opinion based on our experience of having the MCFD wrench Bianca from our arms and the time it took us to heal from this trauma. It was very important that we had our baby with us during this healing process. Instead, the undertone we felt from social workers was, *Well, this woman doesn't deserve this baby, so we'll just take her and she can have another,* and later, *Well, you got your baby back, so get over it and leave us to do our job of "protecting" children.*

Obviously, getting this flippant attitude from social workers hasn't shut me up. Far more attention needs to be given to addressing trauma and breaking vicious cycles where families just seem to inherit problems from the generation before. It needs to stop. I'm starting with three clauses in the B.C. Child, Family, and Community Service Act that I'm specifically calling BS on.

The wording changes slightly in each of Canada's provinces and territories, but the essence of their meaning is the same.

The child is taken as a last resort and only if there are no other, less disruptive measures.[22]

Yeah, right. It seems to me that's the *first* thing they do and then let the chips fall where they may. The MCFD assesses the shattered pieces of a poor family and then plots their strategy accordingly.

The MCFD works with the family to keep the child united with their family of origin whenever possible.[23]

I saw absolutely no evidence of this whatsoever. If anything, the actions of social workers were the exact opposite of this directive. Everything they seemed to do was covert, in secrecy, and with no interest in communicating with us in an open dialogue. They seemed to have already made their decision to take Bianca and didn't care at all what taking a two-week-old baby would do to her mother.

… In the best interests of the child.[24]

It makes my blood boil how they interpret this directive. Neither my nor my daughter's words were ever heard or considered by social workers. They seemed to have already written their own narrative of what they thought was in Bianca's best interest, and anything that didn't fit that predetermined narrative was dismissed.

I don't know if it's even possible to have an open dialogue with government people anymore. Everything that comes out of their mouths seems to be shallow "lip service" rehearsed from a previously written script.

It makes me question this notion of "democracy" because, little by little, elections are starting to be less about who best represents their constituents and more about who has the wealth and "friends with money" to fund a winning campaign. Same shit, different pile. That's pretty much how I sum up trying to

---

[22] *Child, Family, and Community Service Act, B.C., Chapter 46 2(b).*

[23] *8(1).*

[24] *4(1) Child, Family, and Community Service Act, B.C., Chapter 46.*

decide who I "gamble" on in each election. And even more questionable is how invasive government should be in a child's life. Kids can't vote. The political and in court arenas that these poor parents find themselves in are not the best places to resolve what's "in the best interest of the child." That's probably why there's no accountability whatsoever.

Ah, but the inner workings and opinions about politics would fill another book altogether—one best written by someone else. I haven't got the stomach for it.

Canadians would provide interesting and colourful content for such a book, of that I'm sure. I say that because just before Christmas 2020, the Grinch arrived in our province. All holiday travel and inside and outside gatherings were cancelled. It was by the provincial premier's orders working with the recommendations of health authorities to address the high number of COVID-19 cases.

Just a couple of weeks after the Grinch's arrival, around New Year's Eve, it was discovered that several of the province's government staffers had gone on holidays outside the country. One such member of the legislature of Alberta was elected in the city of Grande Prairie. She went to Hawaii over Christmas. This politician clearly could not hear the words coming out of her own yap. She justified this Hawaiian trip by saying that she didn't want to break a family tradition of seventeen years. Albertans, furious and confused, could hardly contain their emotions over their lost Christmas from following their government's COVID-19 lockdowns.

Her constituents responded creatively, swiftly, and with integrity. They plastered Hawaiian leis and Christmas cards on trees growing outside her constituency office. On the Christmas cards, they wrote down *their* family traditions they'd missed out on. A huge banner was waiting for her when she returned to Canada with "Aloha" written across it in massive letters. The irony of aloha meaning both "hello" and "goodbye" is appropriate.

At first, the premier of Alberta said the orders were guidelines only. He would reprimand these travelling taxpayer-funded staffers but nothing more. His phones lit up for days. Albertans would not be accepting that as a fair consequence and wanted their tax dollars and future voting power to be the deciding factor. The premier had no choice but to accept resignations. Those Christmas trips from hypocritical politicians would go down in Canadian history as some of the most expensive getaways to beach destinations. It cost these politicians their six-figure salaries as they were forced to resign.

Not a single person was hurt in this demonstration of anger and frustration. Not a single window was broken nor "mob mentality" harm done to person or property. In fact, country and folk singer Matt Masters wrote a jingle about the government staffer's Christmas traditions and posted it on YouTube. This "Hawaiian princess" could dance her way to the unemployment line, just like the rest of us who had lost our jobs during COVID-19, with his catchy little tune.

No other country is like Canada, and I have nothing but faith in the Canadian people. We try to set things right, and I think it's about time that our politicians actually represent us with the same work ethic, integrity, wit, and sense of humour—not just a bunch of puppets on strings, reciting scripted rhetoric on why their party is better than the other one. It wasn't just Alberta's politicians who snuck away during Christmas but politicians across Canada, too. The only thing damaged were egos and bank accounts, as many of them lost their cushy government jobs.

I find it rich how Trudeau can jet-set around the world on our dime, pontificating about his government's triumphs over human rights violations when we have this BS going on in our own child welfare industry.

But how can the federal government possibly do something about each province's delivery of social services if they can't even properly assess the scope of the problem? CPS has a built-in culture of secrecy, and it's splintered beyond all recognition. How can we get our government to hear the pleas of innocent children, taken from loving families, when all we hear these days is "We are all in this together"?

We might all be in the same storm, but we are definitely rocking in different boats. I'm most concerned about the children clinging in terror to a leaky dinghy, sinking with their parents—or without.

CPS is out of control. I honestly think their sick mantra is as simple as this: *Do the most unbelievable things to these parents, so that is precisely what happens. No one believes them.*

Start listening. Start believing.

Because it is a child's God-given right from the moment they're born to be loved. Fortunately, in most cases, it is their biological parents who truly love that baby unconditionally.

This majority of parents should not be represented by the abhorrent few who do harm to their child and are the focus of sensationalized media coverage. Losing a child to CPS intrusion is such a humiliating, stressful, confusing pain, I truly hope reading this book is the closest you ever come to it.

Because if we don't start reining in these people and demanding accountability, the next kids they could be coming for are yours. CPS's power seems limited only by their own creativity. What if someone called on *you* because your child ate "too much sugar" or "was riding their bike on their own"? That stupid call placed by a "concerned citizen" could be the end of your family. "Too much sugar" could be creatively construed as medical neglect, and a normal, right-of-passage "bike ride" could be construed as an unsupervised unwillingness to care for the child. Parents will surely have to be wardens in their own "fancy prisons" and keep their children out of the public eye.

Finally, and I don't think I've said this enough, I truly thank God for answering my prayers in all this. I know God was in that moment when I looked down at my two-week-old grandbaby and her shining blue eyes were staring right back at me. She was the only one in that room with true power, as she had just been delivered to us, from God, fourteen days earlier. She calmly and quietly let me know that everything would be okay.

She was right—for us anyway.

I have never forgotten all the moms I saw in the courthouse, their young hearts broken, facing an uncertain future without their children. I can still hear that horrid wail coming from the bowels of the courthouse corridors.

I'd like to share something I used to say to my daughter when she was a teenager and going through a confusing situation. I would tell her, "God only gives you what you can handle."

She didn't understand me then, but she does now. It was a mother's prayer and a repeated mantra to empower her child. I wanted my daughter to realize that she already had all the tools she needed. We all do. We have a deep reservoir of resilience we can tap into if need be. My daughter used hers. She chose to trust me and Suzanne and, with all of us united as family, believed that a higher power was on our side. She tried to remain calm to do right by her child. It was easier said than done, given all the stress, but she did it. I watched my little girl transform, carried by the dignity of becoming a mother. I saw her dig deep for her strength and witnessed what love can do.

Because if we don't dig deep for our strength, our collective power as a nation, I fear we might wake up one day and find ourselves in some dystopian horror flick where government owns our children, and couples are reduced to mere baby-making machines.

Still think this is far-fetched?

Go ask parents who are grieving the loss of a child who is still alive.

Go ask Suzanne and Jamie and Marilyn.

They will tell you, "We're already there."

Isaiah 11:6: "... and a little child will lead them all."

EPILOGUE

Still confused? Rest assured, you're human. Like I said, our ordeal was so stressful and so fluid, it was hard to keep track of everything coming at us. It started with the "ankle alarm" that the MCFD put on Bianca, in addition to the birth alert red flag they had on my daughter. It was the beginning of many questions, most still unanswered.

It's no wonder that most parents give up under the sheer volume of stress. It should come as no surprise that some parents take their own lives when they realize they will never see their children again.

Marilyn feared losing her daughter to suicide after the death of Delonna. What a sorry place this world would be to lose a kind soul like Jamie. It's bad enough Delonna Sullivan is no longer here; today, she'd be ten years old.

Suzanne was somehow able to make her way back to living again after Teddy and Derek were taken from her. I'm so glad she did. I honestly don't know what we would've done without her.

She and I did disagree about naming social workers, though, when I was writing this book. I feel it's the system that is pure BS, but Suzanne feels it's both. My husband agrees with her. They feel that it's both the broken system and the manipulative personalities who are protected within it. I decided not to name names—in this edition anyway. After all, it is *my* book..

Taxpayer dollars are used to pay social workers, so most findings *should* be a matter of public record. I'd be well within my right to name names. After Delonna died, her mother was threatened with $10,000 in fines and jail time if she spoke about her daughter dying in foster care. Jamie didn't give a shit. They had taken everything from her. She would go to jail if that's what it took to grieve her daughter and talk about her. Jamie and her mother got a lawyer to help file an application with the courts to have the publication ban on Delonna Sullivan lifted. They won. It wouldn't bring their baby back, but at the very least, they could speak about her to anyone who would listen.

On that day many years ago, at the child protection forum, I listened. I think now Canadians are at that same stage. They are listening to First Nations who've been saying, for years, that there are unmarked graves on the grounds of former Indian Residential Schools.

Is it time for Canadians to unite and to lead its leaders? I think it is.

I think if we put our heads together, in open, honest dialogue, any solution we come up with collectively will be far better than anything I can do on my own. Like I said, I'm just one grammy who's writing a book. I think Canadian moms, dads, grandparents, aunties ... all are far better equipped to start asking *What's in the best interest of the child?*

For trusting me with their stories, I thank my daughter, Suzanne, Michelle, Jamie and Marilyn. I know I can't get back what was lost, but I hope my words have provided some small measure of justice.

Hats off to my husband, too. It turns out, he is a pretty good editor.

Suzanne's only recourse is that the day Derek turns eighteen, she can start looking for him and his brother. Hopefully, they will have some faint memory of her.

Someday, I'd like to meet Michelle in person and her two beautiful children who she fought so hard to keep.

Someday soon, I will visit Jamie and visit her daughter's grave.

We have to let these precious babies know, in this life or the hereafter, that they are not forgotten.

We cannot let them disappear.

Made in the USA
Monee, IL
01 November 2021